BAROQUE AND
ROCOCO ARCHITECTURE

THE GREAT AGES OF WORLD ARCHITECTURE

ROMAN *Frank E. Brown*

GOTHIC *Robert Branner*

BAROQUE AND ROCOCO *Henry A. Millon*

MODERN *Vincent Scully, Jr.*

In Preparation

GREEK *Robert L. Scranton*

EARLY CHRISTIAN AND BYZANTINE *William MacDonald*

MEDIEVAL *Howard Saalman*

RENAISSANCE *Bates Lowry*

ISLAMIC *John Hoag*

CHINESE AND INDIAN *Nelson Wu*

PRE-COLUMBIAN *Donald Robertson*

BAROQUE & ROCOCO ARCHITECTURE

by Henry A. Millon

GEORGE BRAZILLER · NEW YORK · 1961

All rights reserved.
For information address the publisher,
George Braziller, Inc.
215 Park Avenue South
New York 3, New York.

Library of Congress Catalog Card Number: 61–15492

Printed in The Netherlands

Second Printing

CONTENTS

INTRODUCTION

The seventeenth century saw the founding of the modern "absolute state" and the dissolution of the fragmented allegiances of the previous century. The developing concept of an autocratic monarchy tended to vest all power in the hands of a single ruler, who was able to oversee the total organization of a nation and direct it toward a single goal. Since France was the first nation to reap the benefits of absolutism, European history of the seventeenth and eighteenth centuries is largely concerned with French expansionist policy and the efforts of various international alliances to thwart French desires. For two centuries France was the political, social, and economic heart of Europe.

In the scientific realm, during the seventeenth century the varied and independent scientific discoveries of the Renaissance were synthesized into a coherent whole. The synthesis based on the Descartian development of the scientific method was characterized by the invention of projective geometry, calculus, and the development of astronomy. The newly enlarged view of the universe was applied to the newly developed state.

Art and architecture had a new role. They were, in many cases, executed to popularize what were believed to be visible truths about both the Church and the State. Art of the seventeenth and eighteenth centuries was to a large degree an orthodox, persuasive art that at times verged on high-powered propaganda. Art of the Renaissance was, on the other hand, primarily religious, and was relatively simple, self-contained and self-sufficient. More than in the Renaissance, the seventeenth and eighteenth centuries dealt with secular public art in terms of large decorative ensembles designed to display the glory of the patron. But this does not mean that religious art was in any way neglected as is sometimes stated. The earliest and strongest enunciations of seventeenth-century principles are found in church façades and interiors.

BAROQUE

The Renaissance building exists to be admired in its isolated perfection. The Baroque building can only be grasped through one's experiencing it in its variety of effects. Renaissance space is static, its walls and vaults are planal—they form space. Renaissance unity is achieved through a cumulative addition of clearly defined similar static elements, while Baroque unity is achieved—at the expense of the clearly defined elements—through the subordination of individual elements to invigorate the whole. Baroque space is independent and alive—it flows and leads to dramatic culminations. Walls and vaults of Baroque buildings are liberated from the plane surface and interact vigorously with both interior and exterior space.

The essential contrasts can be better grasped through a comparison of the Renaissance church of S. Maria della Consolazione at Todi and the Baroque church of SS. Martina e Luca in Rome (plates 1, 2). S. Maria della Consolazione (begun in 1508 by an unknown designer) is, in plan, a simple domed square with four semicircular apses, i.e., a Greek-cross plan (plate 3). It stands free, on a platform, on a level piece of ground and the exterior mass form is a uniformly dressed masonry envelope conforming precisely to the shape of the interior space. The square crossing is defined by pairs of pilasters at right angles at each of the four corners, and also by the transverse arches, pendentives, drum, and dome. Nothing is hidden—the forms are stated in their purity. The apses are extensions of the square. They appear added to it as if pasted on. They are separate and distinct.

SS. Martina e Luca (designed by Pietro da Cortona in 1635) is also a Greek-cross plan with semicircular apses but the arms are longer than at Todi (plate 4). The façade is independent of the mass and space behind it and follows its own rules of composition (plate 2). From the entrance, the worshiper's gaze is immediately drawn to the main altar. The mass form of the church is not clear from the ground to the lantern. It changes at each string course, and the exterior is less indicative of the interior space than the Todi church. In a sense, the interior and exterior are independent, following different rules and having different aims. SS. Martina e Luca was never intended to be seen in the round. The façade is very different both in form and material from the other three apse ends. It stands two stories high, is made of travertine instead of brick, and is considerably wider than the nave.

In the interior of Todi, the planal walls are articulated by architectural members (plate 5). Doors and windows are clearly and simply cut into the wall surface with a liberal amount of wall area on all sides of the puncture. The resultant classical light reveals all the elements impartially. The architectural membering is a screen that is applied to the planal wall surface to supply an intellectual subdivision of the wall surface into harmoniously related proportional parts. The interior of SS. Martina e Luca is also bathed in light but, other than the openings in the half-dome of the main apse, no windows are visible (plate 6). There are windows at the lower level in the transept arms, in the apse hemicycles, in the drum, and in the lantern, but they are hidden from view. As a result, the brilliantly lighted pilasters and columns fix the attention. The surface is in vigorous relief. The corners at the crossing are beveled, blurring a sharp division into separate parts and creating a more dominant central emphasis. Strong pilasters, arches, and ribs define the arms and divide the crossing from the arms. The wall surface is difficult to determine. Even when the wall does show itself from between burgeoning masses, it is ruptured by a niche that presses against the pilaster on either side. The main sensation is that of powerful massive structural members purposefully describing a strongly conceived space and not simply subdividing a wall surface.

ROCOCO

The architecture of the early eighteenth century began to show some fundamental changes from the blustery assured building of the Baroque. Where Baroque walls, piers, and columns had been massive and forceful, the space focused but divided into parts, and the light variable and dramatic, buildings of the first half of the eighteenth century were, on the contrary, airy and restrained; space was unified, subdivided, and diffuse; and daylight was everywhere abundant and revealing.

These distinctions are best seen by contrasting Cortona's SS. Martina e Luca, already discussed, with Bernardo Vittone's S. Chiara in Bra (plate 7). The comparison will demonstrate the profound alterations in space concept as well as the nature of the mass form of the wall-pier-column structure.

S. Chiara (begun 1742) has a circular plan with four less-than-semicircular lobes added at the cardinal points. The circular center is defined by four piers with paired composite pilasters that lead up to a dome which covers only the central area. The four lobe-chapels extend the central space into large nichelike areas whose exact dimensions are not perceptible (plate 8).

There is a gallery completely encircling the building at the upper level above the chapels. The exterior wall of the gallery supports a second exterior dome that covers the entire church. The area between the two domes is lighted by dormer windows unseen from below. The entire interior is painted in pale subtle colors. Paintings on the under surface of the second dome, illuminated by the dormer windows, show through irregularly shaped perforations of the interior dome. In effect, there are two separate buildings—one set inside the other—that flow together at certain points (plate 9). Contrary to the obvious but homogeneous lighting effects found in the Renaissance church at Todi and the hidden but equally homogeneous light in Cortona's church in Rome, in Vittone's S. Chiara all the main freestanding architectural members that describe the central space are backlighted and are separated from the exterior shell. Backlighting makes those members seem to be part of a slender, lithe structural system internal to the building within a continuous space.

The parts are no longer clearly defined as they are at Todi and in SS. Martina e Luca. The interior dome is pierced by arches that span each of the pier-column groups of the drum region and is still further perforated by the irregular, triangle-shaped peepholes. The domes above the gallery expand the space as they flood it with light. In contrast to both Todi and SS. Martina e Luca, S. Chiara at Bra as it rises is voluminous, airy, and active. What is, at the ground level, a simple circular space continuous with that of the chapels, becomes, at the gallery level, a complex spatial experience with screening columns, hidden light sources, illusionistic effects, double domes, and unseen but implied spaces.

In the early eighteenth century in Italy, France, and Germany, dramatic spatial sequences or complex interwoven spaces were replaced by spaces unified in both vertical and horizontal directions. The Renaissance-Baroque horizontal division into definable areas was replaced by structure that, through its continuity from floor to peak of vault unified the space in the vertical dimension (as in Late Gothic structure) and destroyed the predominantly classical, horizontal qualities of Renaissance-Baroque buildings. Horizontally, interior space was extended unbroken from the entrance to the choir and from exterior wall to exterior wall across the nave and side aisles. In churches the vaulting of the side aisles was often carried up to the height of the nave vault (again as in Late Gothic hall churches), producing a single uniformly shaped space from wall to wall. Intervening structure became a mere skeleton that acted to veil certain portions of the space and punctuate it at vital points. The differences in space, mass, light, structure, and decoration found in the eighteenth-century buildings, when compared to their seventeenth-century counterparts, disclose a new attitude towards architectural space and mass that will, in this volume, be called the Rococo, even though the term was originally coined to characterize a type of decoration invented in France by Pierre Le Pautre at Marly during the early years of the eighteenth century.

story central section flanked by lower set-back, three-story wings of three bays each (plate 19). It is conceived as a bold integration and reinterpretation of aspects of Bramante's "House of Raphael" and Michelangelo's Capitoline palace. As in Bramante's palace the building is clearly divided into the utilitarian ground or service floor, having little architectural treatment, and the upper or living floors that are graced by pilasters, colonnettes flanking the windows, alternating pediments, and rich moldings. Unlike Bramante's scheme, the two top floors of the palace are unified within a single order, as in the Capitoline palace of Michelangelo, and flank the central seven bays by subsidiary wings. The subordination of certain parts to the whole and the linking together of others produces a singularly unified scheme of surprising dignity and power. The palace was so successful it virtually became the standard urban palace solution throughout Europe for the next hundred and fifty years.

Bernini's masterpiece of church architecture, S. Andrea al Quirinale (1658) (plates 20, 21), is an example of convincing, religious theatricalism in which he has also exploited his powers as a sculptor and dramatist. A section of the street before the oval church is drawn into the site by curved arms that frame a convex central portico reminiscent of Cortona's S. Maria della Pace. Once he has passed through the austere entrance the spectator is transported into luxurious gilt and colored-marble surroundings with a dramatically lighted step-by-step story of the martyrdom of St. Andrew. The main altarpiece, supported by stout *putti* and lighted from a hidden source, depicts the martyrdom itself. Above, on the lip of the cornice, supported by a cloud, St. Andrew, after the martyrdom, is being wafted to the heavens (the lantern) toward which he gazes adoringly and from which light falls toward him. S. Andrea al Quirinale is, perhaps, the high point of the Italian Baroque vision fusing as it does painting, sculpture, architecture, and stage design into a totally integrated system.

The wide variety of expression inherent in the Baroque can best be understood by examining, from among the many extraordinary figures that proliferated during the century, the works of Francesco Borromini (1599–1666) and Guarino Guarini (1624–83), as well as those of Bernini. Although Bernini was a phenomenally gifted and versatile artist, his purely architectural works are not of the same stature as those of Borromini and Guarini who were the most original architects of the century. Borromini

SEVENTEENTH CENTURY

As Spanish influence began to wane towards the end of the sixteenth century, Italy experienced a general regeneration of its powers that paralleled the Church's newly regained confidence in spiritual matters. Post-Reformation Italy, prey to mysticism and mortification as taught by Spain, built little. But gradually it reasserted itself and developed an assured, newfound energy that was to transform most of the major cities of Italy.

In Rome, still the religious center of Christendom, and still one of the most powerful of the independent Italian states in the late sixteenth and seventeenth centuries, there were two major architectural works still to be undertaken. The first, and most obvious, was completing St. Peter's (still without façade or dome) and reworking the casual area in front of it. The second was revamping the city to provide for the greatly increased resident population and the ever-increasing numbers of pilgrims.

Since Michelangelo's death in 1564 little work had been done on St. Peter's, but when the energetic Pope Sixtus V was elected (1585) he immediately set to work to complete it. He had men working day and night and on holidays, and the dome was completed in twenty-two months. Only the façade and piazza remained to be constructed.

Paul V finally ordered the remains of the old basilica torn down in 1605. In 1606 Carlo Maderno (1556–1629) won a competition held for the new façade, and by 1612 it was completed (plate 10). Even in a collaborative endeavor Renaissance and Baroque differences were clearly discernible, and Maderno's additions were quite different from Michelangelo's designs. In Michelangelo's scheme the central dome dominated and absorbed all—all spaces and masses, though sharply defined, were contributory to the central dome. The mass of the walls was given new meaning as Michelangelo shaped the exterior wall surface without any real reference to interior space.

Maderno, on the other hand, was working to suggest a fluid, dramatic, dynamic space. The new nave was given windows for light—it was made a bit higher and wider—and the arches separating the chapels down the side aisles were completely eliminated (only the pediment remains). The result was a lighter, airier nave in which space flowed freely from chapel to chapel in the side aisles and from the side aisles into and through the nave (plate 11). On the exterior Maderno continued the rhythmic proportions and sizes that had already been determined by Michelangelo (plate 12). But on the façade he changed Michelangelo's order of pilasters to columns, and, as he had done in the façade of S. Susanna (plate 13) a few years earlier (1597–1603), he varied column rhythm and wall relief to create a dynamic focus and subordinated parts to the whole to achieve unity and direction. Maderno's revolutionary concepts both in terms of fluid interior space and vigorous handling of mass formed the foundation upon which the later masters of the Baroque were to build.

The façade completed, the piazza in front remained to be organized (plate 14). Sixtus V had already placed an obelisk in the square as he had done in other squares throughout the city. An incredible desire for action and accomplishments led him to remake the face of Rome by pushing through wide avenues usually terminating in piazzas at the major pilgrimage centers. In a number of these piazzas he placed obelisks to act as visual foci or nodes within the city. In front of St. Peter's he erected an obelisk that formerly stood to the south of St. Peter's on the spine of the Circus of Nero. The obelisk and a fountain erected by Maderno determined, to some extent, the size, character, and even the approximate location of the piazza. The square had, as yet, no precise limits since at that time it was defined by little other than the papal palace to the north and the *borgo* to the east and south.

Notwithstanding the energy of Sixtus V the piazza was still an ill-defined sprawling area at his death. In 1656 Alexander VII asked Bernini to prepare designs for the piazza. Bernini suggested a practical and yet majestic solution that made it possible to realize an adequately large piazza that could center the main portion on the obelisk already in place, utilize Maderno's fountain, define the piazza by two elliptical colonnades that separated the city from the open space, and form a splendid forecourt for the church (plates 15, 16). In spite of the amount of time which elapsed between the completion of the church and the construction of the piazza, and in spite of the fact that Bernini's colonnade was, strictly speaking, an afterthought, the successful integration of piazza and church almost dwarfed

Maderno's achievement. The piazza is a church square, oriented to the church rather than to the city. Although the east end of the piazza is related directly to the *borgo*, there is no relation of transverse axis of the oval to the street pattern of the city.

A similar indifferent attitude to city-wide circulation is evident also in smaller, more intimate Baroque piazzas. The piazza and façade built in 1656–57 by Pietro da Cortona (1596–1669) for the church of S. Maria della Pace in Rome is an excellent example of the typical small, carefully circumscribed, intimate piazza (plates 17, 18). Cortona's task was to add a modern façade to an existing church and to design a piazza to enclose the façade. Three streets led into the site at irregular angles. Cortona composed the façade so as to create dramatic views, when seen either through narrow doorways in close proximity to the projecting portico or down a narrow street, disclosing only a portion of the appealing façade. The façade itself steps forward boldly at ground level and is artfully counterbalanced at the upper level by the concave wings on either side. The concave wings further act as a foil to the erect central portion of the façade that has within its elements a much subtler repetition of the fluid sequence just described. The streets that enter the square do so through doorways that appear to lead directly into the church. Consequently, the spectator is immediately thrust into contact with the church and is both invited and required to participate. The effect is totally different from that of St. Peter's square. Cortona's square is intimate, restrained, and small. Bernini's square is stately, majestic, and immense.

Gian Lorenzo Bernini was by far the most versatile master of the Baroque. He has been called the Michelangelo of the seventeenth century for while primarily a sculptor he was also a painter, architect, poet, stage designer, and dramatist, as well as the major teacher of the succeeding generation. His fame grew to such bounds that in 1665 Louis XIV invited him to prepare designs for the contemplated new Louvre in Paris. Certainly not since Michelangelo had any artist possessed, to the same degree, the admiration, acclaim, and esteem of popes, princes, artists, and citizens.

While preparing the preliminary designs for the Louvre (which was never begun), Bernini was also designing a palace, which still exists today in Rome, for the Cardinal Flavio Chigi, a relative of Pope Alexander VII. The palace, which dominates the long side of a rectangular piazza, consists of a seven-bay, three-

was, in many ways, the spiritual father of Guarini. Born in Canton Ticino in the Alps, he came early to Rome where he remained for his entire life. Suspicious, moody, and dedicated, Borromini, almost fanatical in his pursuit of perfection, carefully supervised all the stages of his designs, from the models and drawings to the completed structure. The exact opposite of Bernini, the courtier and politician par excellence, Borromini was stubborn, proud, and introverted. Bernini was the inheritor, upholder, and prime exponent of tradition while Borromini was the revolutionary figure with a phenomenal knowledge of all aspects of his craft whose originality had ultimately far greater influence on the course of architecture in western Europe.

Borromini's ecclesiastical work began at St. Peter's. After working for years as an apprentice under his uncle, Maderno, on the completion of St. Peter's, Borromini received in 1638 a commission to design a small church for the Trinitarian order. The church, S. Carlo alle Quattro Fontane, is a provocative reinterpretation of a centrally planned church. The oval dome is placed over a modified Greek-cross plan (plate 22) which has its long axis running from entrance to main altar. The dome is supported on four broad-footed pendentives which are themselves supported by pairs of fully-round columns (plates 23, 24). The longitudinal direction is reinforced by a semicircular apse and entrance bay while the cross arms are portions of flattened ovals. The niches, panels, doorways, and moldings that articulate and activate the wall surface are lighted by hidden windows in the base of the dome. The resulting rich wall surface flows from oval to oval, merging the whole into a fluid mass that defines an intensely dynamic space. S. Carlo marks the first reappearance, since Hadrianic times, of a completely undulating wall surface.

Borromini's superb achievement at S. Carlo is only equaled by the chapel of S. Ivo in Collegio della Sapienza, also in Rome, which was begun in 1642 (plate 25). Seen from the courtyard, the upper regions of the chapel bulge upward and break out into a lantern in strong relief which finally culminates in a curious spiral. The mass form is very carefully composed. Stable pilaster bunches, which appear to contain the volume against internal pressures, lead upward to buttresses which lead, through their forceful curves, to the base of the lantern. There paired columns of the lantern continue the lines to the vertical decorative elements at the base of the spiral. The spiral culminates in an open, wrought-iron bulbous shape that captures and halts the upward movement. The billowing exterior of the church shows strength and vitality but the complex of dome, lantern, and pinnacle is a masterly synthesis of fluid, linear elements and rounded massive elements.

The interior of S. Ivo is a single unified space. The plan is geometrically derived from the superposition of two equilateral triangles to form a regular hexagon. Three sides of the hexagon develop into semicircular apsidal shapes, while the other three sides terminate in convex walls that reverse the curve of the apses (plate 26). The main apse receives strong directional emphasis because it is matched, at the entrance, by only the narrow wall with a reverse curve. The walls are articulated by pilasters, and at the point of intersection of wall surfaces there are always pilasters with crisp, sharp corners that run uninterruptedly from floor to cornice. There is no drum. In an attempt to gain vertical continuity Borromini has rejected the insertion of elements that would emphasize horizontality (pendentives and drum). There is a strong linear continuity from lantern to pavement, interrupted only by the pronounced horizontal of the cornice.

As in S. Carlo, light comes in only above the cornice, but unlike S. Carlo, at S. Ivo six large windows in the base of the tall dome provide ample light to bathe the originally monochromatic interior with an abundant, even light (plate 27). Like S. Carlo, but unlike Bernini's S. Andrea al Quirinale, S. Ivo is rich in forms and ideas but limited in its use of color, choice of materials, and dramatic emphasis. S. Carlo and S. Ivo are buildings that, due to their appeal to the intellect (and their appeal to a completely different aspect of the senses than Bernini's buildings), have concealed within them an ever so subtle, but nonetheless profoundly convincing statement of Borromini's mystical religious beliefs.

Guarino Guarini is the only architect who developed the expressive power of structure and space to even greater degrees than Borromini. Guarini, a priest, mathematician, dramatist, and theologian, was born in Modena. A tormented genius who suffered from near paranoia, he constantly complained of being mistreated, misunderstood, and unappreciated. But he was, without question, the most inventive and original architect of the last half of the seventeenth century.

After teaching mathematics and philosophy in Modena,

Messina, and Paris, in 1666 Guarini went to Turin where he stayed for the remainder of his life. The appearance in small provincial Turin of this monk-of-the-world, man of science, and architect extraordinary, produced a reaction which was felt for several centuries. Within a few years of his arrival his vital creative activity gave the city an architectural life that made it second to none in Italy and gave it an architecture that was structurally and aesthetically in advance of most of the rest of Europe. In the seventeen years remaining in his life, Guarini revolutionized spatial concepts and structural procedures, most particularly with his S. Lorenzo (1666–79), the Chapel of the Sudario (1667–96), and his Church of the Immaculate Conception (1672–97).

In S. Lorenzo, Guarini gave the Piedmont its first (and Italy its finest) late Baroque church. The complex but essentially logical geometry of its plan, its astonishingly successful structural system, and its fascinating, intricately interwoven succession of spaces immediately made it an architectural landmark. In plan the church is composed of four spaces: a narthex as wide as the church; a nave, inscribed in a square; an oval choir; and an annular vault behind the choir (plate 28). At the corners and at the center of each side of the square nave the massive walls bay inward vigorously as if seeking to occupy the space. The space, however, presses back forcefully as if seeking to sap the wall at the lower level (plate 29). The momentary precarious balance of these prodigious forces of space and mass achieved by Guarini at the lowest level of the nave leads to the complete victory of space above in the revolutionary dome and lantern. The dome (plate 30) is an interlaced network of eight slender ribs. At the intersections of the ribs there are, instead of a web, only space and light. Where mass should appear to strengthen the structure Guarini adroitly places a well-lighted hole. Space flows around and through the intersecting ribs. The structure and lighting effect of the dome of S. Lorenzo mark a complete change of direction in Italian church architecture.

The dome, a massive structural entity as conceived by Brunelleschi, Bramante, Michelangelo, and Bernini, was intended (if iconographical significance is disregarded) to be either the chief arbiter of interior space—as in the Pantheon—or the chief element in exterior mass composition—as in St. Peter's. For Guarini, however, the dome was dematerialized and defined but did not limit interior space.

21

The Palazzo Carignano (1679–92) confirmed the versatility, ingenuity, and virility of Guarini's creative powers (plates 31, 32). The large sweeping curves, the assured massiveness, the active surface in high relief, the playing with delicate and massive light and shadow, and the phenomenal control of detail mark the Carignano as undoubtedly the finest late seventeenth-century palace in Italy. The interior of the palace is notable for two reasons: the main staircase and the pierced vaulting of the main salon (plates 33, 34). The evolution of the Italian palace stairway, from its utilitarian, asymmetrical placement in the Palazzo Medici-Riccardi in the early Renaissance to a stately axial, balanced composition, reached its culmination in the Palazzo Carignano. At the Carignano a carefully considered sequence of light and dark, open and closed spaces directs the visitor to the main salon.

As seen from the piazza, the broad sweeping curves of the façade of the palace are ruptured, allowing a bit of the interior to bulge outward at the entrance. Entering the palace through the bulge the visitor finds himself in a small dark vestibule, where guards stood originally, which leads beyond into a half-lighted oval atrium which opens out onto the courtyard. The long side of the oval is parallel to the façade and perpendicular to the entrance. The long axis leads on either side to a few steps that enter a well-lighted rectangular vestibule. Up to this point no main staircase has been in evidence. From either vestibule, however, convexly curved treads of the duplicate main stairs flow through a stair hall that is lighted only by windows at a landing which is halfway up the flight. At the landing the treads reverse their curvature and become both welcoming and inviting. At the top of the flight there is a tall, rich, extremely well-lighted vestibule (directly above the entrance) before the main salon. A circuit is completed. The logic of the exterior and interior forms is clear. The vestibule leads into the most spectacular late-seventeenth-century grand salon in Italy.

Guarini's most influential church design, the church of the Immaculate Conception in Turin for the Mission of St. Vincent de Paul was begun in 1672 (plates 35, 36). A longitudinal church, based on two circles that do not quite intersect, with an undulating façade, the Immaculate Conception church is unusual in that there is no crossing—no domed focus. As a further indication of an intended diffusion of emphasis, the spaces formed, with the exception of a small, domed choir, are identical at entrance and apse. It is a double-ended church. There are no transverse ribs. The ribs all spring either toward the center of the two circles, or, in the case of the area between the circles, spring on a diagonal toward the crown of the vault. The result is a remarkable interweaving of spaces that would normally be thought impossible in a longitudinal church. The walls curve strongly in arcs of circles, the ribs lean inward and outward. The space, although violently shaped, is not interrupted but merges into an incredibly dynamic and expressive entity. This building had far-reaching consequences in Austria and Germany where Guarini's ideas were more fruitfully developed than in any other region.

EIGHTEENTH CENTURY

In the eighteenth century the same economic centers flourished, but Turin as the capital of the kingdom of Savoy was becoming the major power in Italy. Vittorio Amedeo II of Savoy was made the King of Sicily at the end of the War of the Spanish Succession and in 1720 became King of Sardinia. The Savoys spent the remainder of the century consolidating their position in northern Italy.

The family ties between the French rulers and the kings of Savoy resulted in considerable French influence in Italy, but there was also a very strong indigenous development. Furthermore, the holdings of the Holy Roman Empire in northern Italy stimulated interest among the native Italians in the accomplishments of the Austrian and German architects. Rome was still, however, a strong power in central Italy and experienced a remarkable rebirth in the first half of the eighteenth century as French power was lessened.

The spectacular flowering of the Rococo that occurred in Rome from 1725–45 was presaged in the much earlier work of Alessandro Specchi (1668–1729), whose remarkable curvilinear designs for the Porta di Ripetta (1703), now destroyed, on the river at the foot of Via Condotti, disclosed a new feeling for character of line and curvilinear form (plate 37). His designs for the Spanish Stairs (1723) were altered in execution by Francesco de Sanctis but they defined a new direction in terms of space composition (plate 38).

Filippo Raguzzini (c. 1680–1771), chief papal architect to Benedict XIII, carried on with the concepts developed by Specchi. Raguzzini's masterpiece of urban design, his Piazza S. Ignazio (plates 39, 40), which is no wider than the church façade, presents a curiously stagelike character to the viewer as he leaves the church. The façades of the buildings opposite the church are all based on elegant curves derived from ovals. The suggestion of unseen spaces behind the strongly curved buildings causes this piazza to be psychologically more integrated with the city than the preceding examples. There are a few other works by Raguzzini in Rome which he did before the death of Benedict XIII. Among these the most notable is the façade of S. Maria della Quercia (1727) which, with its restrained bayed-out façade, rich surface decoration, and developed pattern of light and shadow, is one of the high points of Roman Rococo (plate 41). Raguzzini is, however, only one example, perhaps the greatest, of a very powerful Rococo school that operated in Rome in the 1730's and 1740's.

A more vigorous aspect of the Rococo can be most clearly seen in the work of Domenico Gregorini (1700–77) and Pietro Passalacqua (?–1748). The massive swelling façade of S. Croce in Gerusalemme (plate 42), one of the finest in Rome, was designed by Gregorini and Passalacqua. It is a bold composition of light and dark accents. The particular quality of the façade is maintained by the studied placement of the openings both in terms of exterior composition and the effect they have on the delightful oval narthex.

Outside Rome the early Rococo can be seen in the works of Filippo Juvarra (1678–1736) who was, surely, the greatest architect in Italy in the early eighteenth century. Juvarra was born in Messina and trained in Rome where he proved to be the most adept pupil of the aging Carlo Fontana. Recognized as one of the most promising architects of the new generation, he was appointed Royal Architect to the new king of Sicily in 1714 and promptly moved to Turin. There he immediately began work on all the major architectural projects of the Savoy rulers. Success followed success and his fame spread throughout Europe. He traveled widely, visited England, and received commissions from both the king of Portugal (1719) and the king of Spain (1735).

The Carmine in Turin (1732), one of Juvarra's last churches, is the finest early Rococo church in Italy (plate 43). A longitudinal church with three chapels and galleries on either side, it has an attenuated structural system with internal piers that are slender and graceful, not in the least massive. The result is a unification of space from exterior wall to exterior wall and from floor to vault in both the nave and side aisles.

The most accomplished eighteenth-century hunting palace in Italy was built by Juvarra for Vittorio Amedeo II at Stupinigi near Turin from 1729–33. The extended sequence of varied exterior spaces (plate 44) that are experienced in arriving at the palace has no equal in Italy and is closely related to ideas current in France that led to the work of Héré de Corny at Nancy. At Stupinigi, Juvarra showed the same tendencies towards unification of space and skeletalization of internal structure that he did in the Carmine. In the domed grand salon (plate 45) an oval space defined by the exterior walls is delightfully punctuated by the slender piers and undulating balcony railing. The effect of the attenuated structural system that denies massiveness is further accentuated by the abundance of light and by the painted decoration with high-value, high-intensity hues placed against a white background. Juvarra's real achievement is in the realization of light, airy spaces bathed in uniform, all-revealing light that merge one into the other to produce an elegant, graceful whole.

The Turinese, Bernardo Antonio Vittone (1702–70), a pupil of Juvarra in Turin and the only outstanding architect in Italy during the middle third of the century, studied also at the Accademia di San Luca in Rome. He was an irritable, cantankerous tyrant who never paid his assistants and never received a major royal commission even though he had no equal in Italy. In his work he was chiefly inspired by Guarini (whose *Architettura Civile* he edited for publication) and Juvarra. From Guarini, Vittone took complicated structural systems creating active but interdependent spaces having great expressive power. From Juvarra, Vittone took attenuated structure, fluid spaces, and an extensive decorative vocabulary. These apparently antithetical aspects were completely transmuted once combined by Vittone. His buildings constitute a new direction—a new attainment with an intensified emotional appeal.

Vittone's late work, best represented by the central-plan church of S. Michele in Rivarolo Canavese (1759), fifteen miles north of Turin, is, in contrast to his earlier buildings, characterized by interiors with more ample spaces and lighter structure that are flooded with an even, airy, diffused white light, and by exteriors that are more integrated with the environment. In plan S. Michele is an irregular but symmetrical octagon with widened bays at the four cardinal points (plate 47a). There is a long slender choir with two side chapels and an oval sacristy off-center to the right. The entrance is set back from the street and two curved lower pavilions sweep out from the portico and frame it (plate 46). The church becomes a part of the city. The street is temporarily widened to mark the presence of the notable building.

In the interior (plate 47), in its vertical division, S. Michele shows a dome resting on a drum that also serves as a pendentive region. The exciting ambiguities of S. Chiara in Bra in the drum and pendentive regions are replaced in S. Michele by a serene fusion of the two elements into a connective region that emphasizes vertical continuity. Level by level as it rises the church is increasingly filled with light that floats down over pinks, pale blues, light grays and soft greens to the floor below. The effect is one of great delicacy without fastidiousness, and the church is one of the most genuinely captivating works of architecture in the world. Only in the superb Rococo of Southern Germany and Austria were there architects who, working along parallel lines, were able to dissolve the fabric to a greater degree.

3   FRANCE

In the latter half of the sixteenth century France was split by religious conflict. When a Protestant Bourbon king, Henry IV, was to succeed to the defunct Catholic Valois line (1589), open war broke out. Ultimately Henry found it necessary to abjure the Protestant religion to take possession of his capital (1594), but it was not until 1598 at the Peace of Vervins and contemporaneous publication of the Edict of Nantes, granting freedom of religion in France, that he was able to unite all France under a single ruler.

Henry and his minister, Sully, began a calculated series of changes in the governmental structure designed to increase the power of the throne and of the bourgeoisie at the expense of the aristocracy. In this way they hoped to make France once more the greatest single power in Europe. With the accession of Louis XIV, by the middle of the seventeenth century, France was the one power feared by all of Europe and the history of Louis' reign is, in a sense, a history of France's attempt to exploit these fears. The concentration of administrative power in the hands of the King and his ministers enabled the crown to organize the entire country for war and commerce in a rational way. The immediate results of this organization in both political and military terms was obvious in France's continued successes, but it also had a revolutionary effect on architecture. As national wealth was virtually concentrated in the hands of a single person, Louis was, more than any man before him or since, able to build at any scale without thought of expense. His buildings still stand today as epitomies of worldly splendor and magnificence attesting to the virtues of a highly organized state as well as to the munificence of its ruler.

Toward the end of Louis' reign, while the political and economic organization of the state did not materially change, the power of the bourgeoisie was growing even greater. Whereas in the sixteenth and early seventeenth centuries, every major commission, except those from the crown, came from the landed aristocracy, in the later seventeenth century the emasculated aristocracy was forced to live at court and was much less able to commission significant buildings. The history of the architecture of the seventeenth century is primarily concerned with the building projects of the crown, princes of the blood, prime ministers, and the burgeoning bourgeoisie.

The seventeenth century also saw the rise of French Baroque Classicism, a stoic and didactic version of the Baroque. Equally evident in science, philosophy, religion, theater, painting, and architecture, Baroque Classicism is a rational, reserved, and specifically French manifestation. Never before or since has France had, at one time, such an array of mental giants as Descartes, Pascal, Desargues, Corneille, Racine, Molière, Poussin, Claude, and François Mansart. By mid-century the carefully controlled and subtly refined Classical Baroque trend was clearly established. In France its pre-eminent position was never seriously challenged. French Baroque architecture was more restrained in its expression than its Italian counterpart. The French architects were fully cognizant of the principles discovered in Italy, but they were also influenced by traditional French values and chose to limit their architectural vocabulary in accordance with them. Within these self-imposed limits they produced works of great order wherein variety was achieved principally through subtle adjustments in rhythm and proportions of mass and wall surface.

A comparison of a Late Classical Baroque example by Jules Hardouin Mansart (c. 1646–1708) with Cortona's SS. Martina e Luca, previously described, will delineate many notable differences and similarities between French and Italian solutions. The church of Les Invalides in Paris (1680–91) is J. H. Mansart's most massive and yet most rhythmical and dynamic composition. As in Cortona's church there is a strong directional emphasis even though Les Invalides stands free to be seen on at least three sides (plate 48). At the entrance, to provide a culminating focus, Mansart steps the façade forward, narrows the intercolumniations, and increases the depth of the relief. The freedom with which he manipulates wall surface and mass, while conceived in more reserved and traditional rectangular terms, is paralleled, in SS. Martina e Luca, by the freedom exercised by Cortona in dealing with massive curved wall surfaces, pilasters and columns.

In plan Les Invalides is a clearly defined Greek-cross with four satellite chapels and a curiously Palladian-like, laterally expanded apse (plate 49). The satellite chapels are reached only through small arched openings that enter from the arms of the cross, and through the center of the four broad piers that define the central space. But the satellite chapels are not really extensions of the central space. The central space is overwhelmingly dominant. In Cortona's church the central space is less dominant, but the wall surfaces are more active and boldly articulated. At Les Invalides columns and entablature define, less vigorously, but more clearly, a central space that is overpowering. Pairs of pilasters parallel to the wall support a single transverse arch while the columns support only an entablature. In SS. Martina e Luca both the column and pier support separate concentric arches that emphasize, in terms of mass, the connection between the arms and the central space. Both interiors strive for integration of the arms and central space—Les Invalides through the clarity of the subordination of the parts—SS. Martina e Luca through the manipulation of massive columns, pilasters, and walls. French classical Baroque architecture of the seventeenth century is, like Les Invalides, characterized by its carefully controlled and restrained forms that are invigorated by a highly developed sensibility to the creative possibilities inherent in traditional solutions.

When Henry IV occupied Paris in 1594 he immediately began to add to the royal buildings and sought to remake Paris to house its recently expanding population. By adding a series of residential squares with uniform façades, Henry hoped both to provide needed living quarters and to transform the medieval character of the city. The new bourgeois squares were an immediate success and were imitated all over Europe.

The three most important and notable architects in seventeenth-century France were Jacques Lemercier (1580/5–1654), François Mansart (1598–1666), and Louis Levau (1612–70). Jacques Lemercier, son of an architect, was sent by his father to Rome where he stayed from c. 1607–14. A favorite of Richelieu, Lemercier was commissioned in 1635 to design the church of the Sorbonne. In plan the church is unusual in that it has two principal entrances: one opening on the courtyard, the other on the piazza in front of the church (plate 50). Lemercier focused these two entrances on the central dome. He unashamedly demonstrated his knowledge of Roman examples since the plan and dome recalled S. Carlo ai Catinari in Rome which was under construction while he was there. But Lemercier's church is more reserved than its Roman model—more refined in its lines and less vigorous. It is a chastened version of the early Roman Baroque.

Lemercier opposed flat decorative planal surfaces to massive vigorous forms in high relief. He demonstrated the full range of his ability when he contrasted the vigorous lower story with six fully round columns (that gains its power from deep shadow and strong highlights) with the almost-flat upper story that is entirely dependent on the precise and delicate adjustments of its architectural members and decorative features, both in depth (to gain delicate shadow lines) and in proportion (to gain a tightly organized and carefully balanced composition) (plate 51). The fully exposed dome rises boldly from the roof of the transept arm. The pilasters, ribs, and lantern delineate the shape of the dome with fluid, graceful lines. Lemercier was at his best in the church of the Sorbonne. The church is, throughout, that rare combination of robustness and delicacy characteristic of all of Lemercier's work. He was a master of delicate elegant line and graceful silhouettes which he ingeniously combined with forceful mass.

In contrast to Lemercier, François Mansart was a difficult person to deal with. A perfectionist, he would spare his client no expense to achieve the effect desired. He often changed plans while the building was under construction and would brook no interference with his ideas. He received few royal commissions. Mansart, who never went to Italy, staunchly developed his own intensely rational, highly polished, and purposefully restrained architecture that virtually determined a national style that was to have profound influence on all succeeding generations even across the borders of France. His pre-eminence among seventeenth-century classical Baroque architects in France is due primarily to his forceful, assured handling of clearly defined mass forms that achieve carefully calculated climaxes.

Ste. Marie de la Visitation, begun in 1632 (plates 52, 53), the earliest of Mansart's churches that show.his developed personality, is a small, restrained, circular domed church with domed oval main and side chapels added on the major axes. A dark entranceway emphasizes the well-lighted chapels. Each of the four domes is lighted by a lantern. Even though chaste and reserved, it is a church that shows a clear subordination of parts to the whole. The oval shapes of the small chapels would, if completed, intersect the circle of the main central space. But, at the cornice level, Mansart retained the purity of the circle and cut into the oval dome of the chapel, subordinating the chapels to it and powerfully integrating them into the total composition.

In the calculated use of lighting and in the effect of interpenetrated space achieved, Mansart showed a complete comprehension of Baroque principles which he, however, chose to employ in more reserved and limited ways. Mansart's exteriors and interiors, composed with scrupulous purity and infinite stability, make him in architecture what Poussin is in painting—the cornerstone of French Baroque Classicism.

In 1634 Gaston d'Orléans commissioned François Mansart to reconstruct the Château at Blois completely. Construction was begun in 1635, and in 1638 it was interrupted. The two constructed wings constitute less than a quarter of Mansart's plan. Mansart confined himself to the use of limestone for the walls and slate for the roofs. He composed his building using only mass, precise and crisp delineation of surface patterns, openings, and light and shadow. In spite of a great economy of means his incredible sensitivity to proportion and relationships of mass produced at Blois a sonorous and assured statement of his principles. The main courtyard entrance through a curved arcade leads into Mansart's astonishing stairwell—the most outstanding feature of the whole château (plate 54). The stairwell is open through three floors. At the second floor the well is partially enclosed to effect a passageway from one side of the building to the other. The passageway defines a rectangular opening through which, from the lower floor, the dome that covers the stairwell can be seen (plate 55).

The exciting spatial play and bold mass composition that Mansart achieved at Blois was developed further in his château at Maisons. In 1642 René de Langeuil, a *nouveau-riche* bourgeois financier, decided to build on his estate a château that would reflect his new position. Mansart was selected as his architect, and the building was completed by 1646. Maisons remains today the most complete example of Mansart's work in terms of both exterior and interior. A careful study of Maisons alone would be a convincing demonstration of his phenomenal abilities and of the influence he was to have on eighteenth-century French architecture. In plan the building is a free-standing block with a central frontispiece and flanking wings of the same height (plate 56). Maisons is the only building in which Mansart's crisp, restrained interior decoration survives almost intact. On the interior as on the exterior of all his buildings, he employs only carved limestone. All of his interiors are conceived in terms of spaces well-defined by white limestone columns, vaults, and walls, which are articulated by finely carved detail without a trace of gilding or painting.

The stairwell at Maisons goes through four flights around the side of a square. As at Blois it is covered with a dome and has a narrow oval gallery at the second level to allow passage from one side of the building to the other. The details of the stair baluster and sculptured decoration are much more restrained than at Blois; and, due to the lack of windows above the second level, the striking effect of the sequence of spaces achieved at Blois is less effective at Maisons. On the exterior, however, the composition is more complex than at Blois and there is much greater emphasis on relief. The central frontispiece, for example, shows the most relief on the first floor at the doorway where it is also narrowest. It is capped by an unbroken entablature. At the second floor it is recessed, the entablature is broken and is easily connected to the top story that is set back to the plane of the wall itself. The pediment above the top story is also broken, but the composition is resolved at the peak where the raking cornice remains unbroken. The whole is a masterfully subtle combination of similar but varied elements.

While Mansart was the major architect at work in France, his obstinacy and individuality made it impossible for him to be included on projects that required a team of architects, painters, sculptors, and landscape designers to work together to produce an integrated whole. Such a team—architect, Louis Levau (1612–70); painter, Charles Le Brun (1619–90); sculptor, Gilles Guerin (1616–78); landscape designer, André Le Nôtre (1613–1700)—whose work was to astound the century by the quality and scope of its integration, collaborated on a grand scale for the first time at the château of Vaux-le-Vicomte. Vaux was the most splendid and important non-royal château in France since it served as the model for Versailles. It was built by Nicolas Fouquet, Louis' Minister of Finance, in 1657–61. Louis XIV and intimate members of the court were invited there for supper on August 17th, 1661. The evening included a presentation of *Les Fâcheux* by Molière with sets by Le Brun, and music by Lully, ending with a fireworks display viewed from the terrace. Louis was so impressed he soon commissioned Levau, Le Brun, and Le Nôtre to expand and redesign Versailles.

Louis Levau, the son of a master mason and probably trained by his father, began his career building town houses for wealthy bourgeois families. Levau's early work, such as the Hôtel

Lambert, with its novel use of the site, ingenious plan, oval and octagonal rooms, and striking main staircase, was evidence of sufficient accomplishment to merit his replacing Lemercier at the Louvre upon the latter's death. Levau showed a sensitivity to the power of Italian examples that was unusual in a French architect. His thoroughly admirable Collège des Quatre Nations (plate 57) is a very personal reinterpretation of Cortona's S. Maria della Pace, and Borromini's and Rainaldi's S. Agnese in Piazza Navona. Vaux-le-Vicomte was, however, his greatest opportunity and perhaps also his greatest success. In plan the château, surrounded by a moat, is a traditional freestanding block articulated by corner and central pavilions (plate 58). But Levau changed the center pavilion to a domed oval salon facing the garden. On the entrance façade, blocks of two bays each step back to the center three-bay arched entrance. The garden façade is the most successful (plate 59). It is a forceful composition of two pavilions with tall angular roofs flanking the robust dome that thrusts out of the main block of the building. But of even greater importance was the decisive relation of garden to château achieved here by Le Nôtre for the first time.

André Le Nôtre, a son of the royal gardner of the Tuileries, was born in Paris and studied both painting and architecture before he settled on landscape design. He was a kind, gentle, impulsive, but unassuming man with a phenomenal breadth of vision and a desire for the integration of buildings, water, plants, trees, and exterior spaces into a single coherent and completely unified scheme. At Vaux, Le Nôtre first used radiating avenues cut through woods or lined with trees; fountains in combination with large planes of water; treeless, wide-open, hedged and planted parterres in contrast to dense wooded areas; and a multiplicity of different terrace levels. The plan of the garden is not as fully developed as his plan for the Tuileries (plate 60), which in 1664–72 replaced the random checkerboard pattern characteristic of the sixteenth century (plate 61), nor as developed as his plan for the gardens at Versailles. Nevertheless, at Vaux there were all the elements he was later to use so successfully. Le Nôtre isolated the château in the center of an open space carefully designed to emphasize the placement of the château. Terraces, parterres, pools, fountains, all provided nodal points with established axial relationships to the château.

It was at Versailles that Le Nôtre found full scope for his genius. The gardens (begun 1667) are a perfect expression of the control over nature exercised by seventeenth-century man (plates 62, 63). Trees were used at Versailles as shadowed masses, in an almost architectural way, to define lighted spaces and to create lengthy vistas. The spaces were punctuated by fountains or paved with long, wide, tranquil pools of water. Polychrome parterres close to the palace led to a grass *allée* bordered by solid masses of trees that extended toward the grand canal. The grand canal continued almost beyond the horizon. A clear view of the axis was never broken. Man had conquered nature and molded it with precision and order from the palace to infinity. The garden at Versailles developed through several stages over a period of years while the château itself expanded vastly. From a small château used as a hunting lodge by Louis' father, Versailles became, under Louis XIV, the seat of his government and the residence for his court. Moreover, it was a tangible demonstration to Frenchmen and the world that absolute power made France the richest and most magnificent country in the world, as well as the most powerful. The final architectural scheme linked together as a unit into one vast enterprise the gardens, palace, and the city to the east.

Levau was commissioned in 1669 to enlarge the earlier château. He was at his best in the garden façade where all the units, though clearly defined, are subordinated to the center where a freestanding portico at the level of the principal floor, in strong relief, breaks the rhythm and establishes a stable focus (plate 64).

Levau was succeeded by Jules Hardouin Mansart, the grand-nephew and pupil of François Mansart. It was he who filled in Levau's terrace between the two flanking pavilions, and greatly extended the building to the north and south, trebling its size (plates 63, 65). On the garden façade of Versailles, he repeated Levau's forms but when the Royal Chapel was added (1698) Mansart allowed full expression of his own abilities. The longitudinal chapel, which ends in an apse the full height and width of the building, is tall and slender with a royal-gallery level (plate 66). The proportions are those of a Gothic chapel. The space is flooded by a liberal amount of light pouring in from tall windows at the ground floor, gallery, and clerestory. Piers and arcades with exquisite decorative detail define the nave and side aisles at the ground floor and effortlessly support the Corinthian columns rising from the gallery level. The remarkable quality of detail and its superb execution with the finest sense of craftsmanship make the chapel a major feature of the château, which itself surpasses all other palaces in Europe for the integration of all the arts and for the sustained level of craftsmanship in all its parts.

As the eighteenth century began, the aging Louis XIV (who was sixty-two in 1700), sensing a lessening of his ability to enjoy various sensual pleasures, developed a greater interest in piety and temperance. Life at Versailles became a dreadful bore, and the young noblemen fled to Paris to form a more exciting society of their own. It is understandable, therefore, that the first manifestations of a rejection of the ponderous dignity of Louis XIV for something light, elegant, gay, and even sometimes playful would emerge in the interior decorations and redecorations of Parisian town houses—such as the Hôtel de Soubise Salon Ovale by Germain Boffrand, c. 1730 (plate 67)—and in the smaller, less formal châteaux. The new attitude (the Rococo) eventually affected architecture, and strong, active, robust interior spaces were rejected in favor of intricate, restrained, and elegant unified spaces. From France the Rococo spread rapidly as far as Russia and the New World. Eighteenth-century French architecture is still regarded today as the ultimate standard of domestic elegance and refinement.

Jacques Ange Gabriel (1698–1782) was the most accomplished architect of the eighteenth century in France. The son of a renowned architect, he was phenomenally successful at an early age. He was responsible for buildings that are the most exquisite combinations of quiet dignity, superb craftsmanship, and elegant proportional relations yet devised by man. The Petit Trianon (1762–64) in the gardens at Versailles, built as an intimate weekend house for Madame Du Barry, is Gabriel's finest residential design and a high-water mark in French architecture. Eighteenth-century architects moved away from the vapid, pompous Louis XIV forms toward dispositions of interior space that emphasized privacy, heretofore ignored, and intimacy, as well as convenience. "Functional" domestic architecture began with Gabriel (plate 68). In contrast to the Château itself, which had no dining room, at the Petit Trianon Gabriel had both a salon and a dining room which opened onto separate terraces. To insure uninterrupted privacy, the dining room table could be set and served at the kitchen below and raised into place. Although in the Petit Trianon Gabriel developed notable technical achieve-

35

ments in prandial elevators and cantilevered masonry stairs and made noteworthy advances in apartment planning, it is in the building's exterior form and its relationship to the gardens that he demonstrated his unquestioned supremacy as an architect. The building is a sharply defined white limestone cubical block with clean-cut edges and straight-forward junctures with the ground and sky. The façades vary according to the interior disposition.

The composition of the west façade has been deservedly admired for generations (plate 69). There is a harmonious emphasis on the central bay and on the stairs that lead to the garden terrace. The central half of the block which projects forward slightly has placed against it four equally spaced columns on bases. The bare walls flanking the central section have, at the ground floor, a single tall window in the center of an ample wall surface. In contrast, the center section seems to be all windows and columns—open instead of closed. The outer sections are bathed in light with only the moldings around the windows and beneath the cornice creating shadows. The central section, on the other hand, is richly articulated by deep masses of shadows under the entablature and delicate linear shadows on the flutings of the columns. Purely through manipulation of mass and light, using only limestone and glass, Gabriel has created a façade of great interest and sophistication. The tranquil harmony of the proportional relations between the bare wall and the center section and between the center section and the entire mass was achieved only through a scrupulous series of subtle and minute adjustments in the size of the elements.

Although crystalline in its purity the façade is also superbly integrated with the gardens. The principal terrace attached to the building is wider than the façade and, as it curves outward, it enfolds the garden and links it inseparably with the façade. As the double stairs descend to the lower terrace they both invite the garden to the terrace and the building into the garden. A full appreciation of the Petit Trianon is not complete without including the garden, composed of *tapis vert* bordered by flower beds and enclosed by clipped masses of trees, which culminates on the main axis in a circular pool. The sophisticated ensemble of palace and garden is a serene and perfectly consonant masterpiece.

Gabriel was selected by Louis XV from among a group of competitors to design a square on the river to the west of the

Tuileries gardens in Paris that was to connect the existing Champs Elysées (at that time a wood) and the projected church of the Madeleine to the north, with the Tuileries. The Place Louis XV (later changed to Place de la Concorde), begun in 1753, was to have, as designed by Gabriel, an equestrian statue in the center of a rectangular *place* oriented perpendicularly to the river. Gabriel's brilliant solution was to create a dry "island" approachable only by bridges that spanned a fifty-foot-wide dry "moat" fourteen feet deep (plate 70).

Subtly refined buildings opposite the river act as screens to close off the end of the square and to define the cross axis. The Place Louis XV is different from Italian squares in many significant respects. In front of St. Peter's, S. Maria della Pace, or S. Ignazio, the space decides the shape of the plan of the buildings. In Paris there is no strongly shaped space. The sides are defined by buildings, by the woods of the Champs Elysées, by the river, and by the Tuileries gardens. The smaller "island" is defined not by buildings but by a moat, balustrades, and sculpture. As it might be in Italy, the focus is defined with a statue and fountains, but in Italy squares are usually inserted within a completely urban environment and are entirely enclosed by buildings. Gabriel's solution shows a remarkable integration of nature and architecture—an integration of a river bank, woods, gardens, statuary, fountains, and urban architecture into a unified scheme. Gabriel's buildings and squares set a standard for official dignity and self-confident majesty that continued to be emulated in various city squares, government buildings, consulates, and upper-class residences until our own day.

The enlargements made in 1751–59 to the city of Nancy, when it became the capital of King Stanislaus Leczinski's domain, constitute one of the most interesting and exciting sequences of spaces in the history of urban design. Energetic and benevolent, King Stanislaus selected as his architect Emmanuel Héré de Corny (1705–63), a native of Lorraine who, as far as is known, never went to Italy or even Paris and, yet, was an outstanding master of eighteenth-century architecture in France.

Héré's task in designing a new Place Louis XV for Nancy was to unite the new town (beyond the fortifications which had recently been demolished) with the old town containing a site for the royal residence. Héré designed what were, in effect, three interconnected squares (plates 71, 72). Within the old city, in front of the new palace, he described with two hemicycles an oval space parallel to the palace, which, opposite the palace, opened on the Place Carrière. The Place Carrière was a long rectangular square with four rows of lime trees down the center. Both a square and a promenade area, the Place was enclosed by residences with uniform façades. At the end of the Place Carrière Héré constructed, at the edge of the moat, a triumphal arch with three openings leading to a bridge. At each corner wrought-iron gates were combined with sculpture groups. The square, now appropriately called Place Stanislaus, is unique in its perfect integration of sculpture, ironwork, and architecture of a sustained high quality.

4   AUSTRIA AND GERMANY

Architecture in Austria and Germany during the seventeenth and eighteenth centuries was greatly influenced by Italian and later by French examples. But, nevertheless, the indigenous Austrian and German achievement of the eighteenth century was of sufficient stature to merit international attention and acclaim.

The seventeenth century had hardly begun when the murder of Henry IV of France removed the one strong stabilizing influence in Europe. Within a decade the League (Catholic) and the Union (Protestant) had begun the Thirty Years War (1619–48) that sapped the strength and resources of all Europe and of Germany and Austria in particular. The Peace of Westphalia brought an end to the war but little stability. The small states that made up Germany and Austria had for the next thirty-five years to resist, to the west, French expansionist policy and, to the east, the increasing pressure of the Turkish armies.

Not until 1683, when the Sultan's armies were decisively defeated at the Siege of Vienna, were there relatively trouble-free times in central Europe. The small nations were faced with the gigantic task of rebuilding what had been destroyed and building anew for a rapidly expanding population. The major urban building was directed to the construction of palaces and churches as in the remainder of Europe; but unlike other west European nations, Germany and Austria in a flood of building activity built (or rebuilt) hundreds of rural monastic establishments. In southern Germany alone, for example, there were over two hundred and thirty churches built between 1700 and 1780. The building spurt had profound influences on the other arts as well, and during that period there were hundreds of fresco cycles and sculpture groups undertaken. Urban buildings were usually paid for by the crown, the nobility, or the state; but, to a large degree, the rural monasteries were paid for by the people themselves.

The abbeys, monasteries, and sanctuaries are not in any way to be considered as structures designed by or for the elite or connoisseur but rather as a popular art springing from the people themselves, built largely for their benefit. Therein lies the explanation for the essential differences between the architecture of the Austrian and German Baroque and Rococo and the sophisticated architecture of France and Italy. In both France and Italy the notable architectural examples were largely the product of the church and the nobility. It is also precisely in this sense that Austrian and German architecture was both astonishingly advanced for its day and, at the same time, retarded. The architecture was advanced in its acceptance and assimilation of the latest Italian and French ideas which were rapidly transformed into a popular and unique expression. But the works were also retarded in that the High Baroque was late in coming to fruition. There is no High Baroque until the 1680's in Austria and hardly any before 1700 in Germany.

The many different manifestations found in Austrian and German art can be explained partly by the fact that it was produced both at the top and the bottom levels of society and partly by the political subdivisions. Central European architecture and decoration was highly varied: it was sophisticated and naïve, aristocratic and popular, refined and crude. It was the last great attempt to achieve a complete synthesis of painting, sculpture, architecture, music, and pageantry. Since that time integration has not been a goal for, as the incentives toward specialization increased, the desire for an integration of all the visual arts diminished. Today we stand openly in awe of—almost unable to comprehend—the profound interrelationships that characterized the eighteenth-century central European concept of order.

The specific character of the central European achievement can best be seen when compared with familiar examples from Italy. The Benedictine Abbey of Ottobeuren in Southern Germany (Bavarian Swabia), an apt example by one of the greatest German masters, has been cited by Caryll Nicolas Powell as the "peak of German rococo attainment." The plans were drawn up by Johann Michael Fischer (1692–1766) in 1744 and the church, his largest, was perhaps also his finest. The pale frescoed vaults are by Johann Jakob Zeiller, and the splendid sculpture is by Johann Michael Feichtmayr. The church is both a reinterpretation of the traditional basilican type and a combination of the basilica and the central-plan church.

The church at Ottobeuren stands to the south of the small village it dominates. The plan is immediately apparent from the exterior—a longitudinal basilica with large transept, crossing, choir, and side chapels on the nave (plate 73). The façade (plate

74), flanked by twin towers, bays out vigorously at the entrance. The interior space is partitioned by piers and vaults into three domed units (nave, crossing, choir) and the vaulted transepts (plate 75). The effect is almost that of a Greek-cross plan. Diagonal piers and broad-footed pendentives at the crossing emphasize its larger dimension (plate 78). White walls highlighted by gilt ornament and the gray and pink marble columns and pilasters are flooded with a brilliant white light from the nave clerestory, the windows in the side chapels, and, above all, from the seven large windows in each of the transepts. The flood of light ripples across the white and gold surfaces, producing an effect of lightness, airiness, and dematerialization. Decorative accents and the highly active forms of the altars with their low-value and occasionally intense hues dominate the white walls and sober architectural membering. At Ottobeuren what is an essentially clearly defined, simple space is animated by a brilliantly lighted surface activity. Far to the south, in Rome, at S. Maria in Campitelli, light is used more dramatically, walls are more active, and the space is a dynamic element. S. Maria in Campitelli is a High Baroque church built by Carlo Rainaldi about a hundred years earlier (1663–67). There are certain similarities between the Rainaldi church and Ottobeuren; in design each building is a combination of central and longitudinal plans with a transverse axis and a domed choir (plates 73, 76). Campitelli is all columns, pilasters, and openings (plate 77). It is a rich, powerful statement of the mass of the building. The space itself is both formed by the building fabric and in turn forms the fabric itself. There is nothing stable—nothing simple. The result is a forcefully directed space that focuses on the dimly lighted apse. Clerestory windows in the nave are small and admit relatively little light. At the choir, however, the clerestory windows are larger and, together with the circle of windows under the dome, admit a great pool of light. The altar is kept in complete darkness and there is consequently a distinct visual progression from partial light, through a well-lighted choir, to the unlighted apse which contains a miraculous icon.

There is neither dramatic focus nor mystery developed at Ottobeuren. The entire church is the experience and it does not present a spatial climax as does Campitelli. At S. Maria in Campitelli sculpture, painting and furniture all have their appointed architectural place in the church within defined frames, while at Ottobeuren the decoration, sculpture and painting float about all over the church converting the whole building into a sacred theater, mixing in among the parishioners, captivating them, and transporting them to a dream world of shimmering light (plate 78).

The degree of integration of the visual arts achieved by the Austrians and Germans was never equaled in Italy, even in the Rococo. Bernard Vittone's S. Maria di Piazza in Turin is one of the masterworks of the High Rococo in Italy, but its appeal is less complete, even if more intellectual. It, too, is a longitudinal church with domed nave and choir (plate 79). Vittone's spaces, when compared with S. Maria in Campitelli, are certainly less dynamic; the wall itself is less vigorous, and the spatial sequence less dramatic (plate 80). The structure is lighter and the surface more highly articulated and decidedly more active. Light is more abundant and more revealing and there is a much greater unification of the spatial units than in the Roman church (plate 81). When compared with Ottobeuren, however, S. Maria di Piazza appears to be a vigorous, powerful statement with dramatic and clearly defined contrasting dynamic spaces. The structure seems heavy and measured, the surface well ordered and carefully modulated with respect to the structure. The light seems restricted and even contrived. In fact the entire church seems to be made up of a series of discrete parts that are in some masterful way knitted into a whole. Ottobeuren, on the other hand, is a superb synthetic whole in which the parts are never separate, the elements never discrete, but the spaces, surfaces, lighting, sculpture, and furniture are all fused into a conceptual unity.

AUSTRIA

The three great masters of Austrian Baroque architecture were Johann Bernhard Fischer von Erlach (1656–1723), Jakob Prandtauer (1660–1726), and Johann Lucas von Hildebrandt (1668–1745). Hildebrandt was born in Genoa, and he studied in Rome under Carlo Fontana. By 1695 he was an engineer for one of the Imperial Austrian armies, and apparently spent time in the Piedmont as well as in Austria. He was appointed Imperial Court Engineer in 1700 and in 1720 was knighted by the Emperor for his accomplishments.

The history of Austrian Baroque architecture is an account of the rivalry and competition between Hildebrandt and Fischer von Erlach, twelve years his senior. Fischer von Erlach also studied in Rome and spent at least five years in Italy. He returned to Vienna in 1687 where he soon became an outstanding success. In 1705, five years after the younger Hildebrandt, he was appointed Imperial Court Architect, a post he held until his death. He was acquainted with the architecture of most of Europe (he traveled to Prussia, Prague, France, England, and Holland, as well as Italy) and in 1712 wrote the first History of Architecture (*Entwurf einer Historischen Architektur*, Vienna, 1721). Fischer's buildings are austere, imposing, and impressively monumental.

Fischer and Hildebrandt, the "educated court architects" have nothing in common with Prandtauer. He was trained in the trade as a craftsman-sculptor and entered the field of architecture only in his forties when he built his first church for an abbot in upper Austria. Much freer and more rhythmical than Fischer von Erlach, he was the first non-urban architect to develop an important personal expression.

Fischer von Erlach's masterpiece of church architecture, the Karlskirche in Vienna, built from 1715 to 1733 in thanksgiving for relief from the great plague of 1713, is an architectural medley of great quality (plates 82, 83). The extremely wide façade, which can be read in a multitude of different ways, is punctuated by small towers, arches, historiated columns, and portico, culminating in the tall drum and dome over the central longitudinal oval. The parts never quite seem to come together, however, and the single static unified space of the interior belies the multiplicity of effects on the exterior. The interior space is focused on the well-lighted main altar at the end of a long, narrow, and relatively dark choir that is contrasted in space form and light character to the wide, tall, openly lighted vertical central space. The resultant dramatic contrast gives a direction and forcefulness to the otherwise somber and austere interior.

Fischer's lack of originality was offset by his immense learning and intelligence. He was a man of contrasts who exhibited knowledge of the latest designs in both Italy and France and yet experimented with Mannerist space conceptions and decorative motifs. The ultimate assessment of Fischer's worth must rest on his influence as well as on his accomplishments. Through his work, Austrians learned that it was no longer necessary to import foreign architects; and Fischer's own architectural achievement became the model for the next two generations of central European architects.

Lucas von Hildebrandt was more of an architect than Fischer though less of an intellect. His early work gave evidence of his attempt to master the latest Italian schemes and to carry them a step further. His Piaristen Church in Vienna (plates 84, 85) owed a great debt to Guarini's S. Lorenzo in Turin but some of the implications of Guarini's building were explored somewhat further. The cornerstone of the church was laid in 1698 but the church was not under construction until 1716. Hildebrandt's walls are active and curve vigorously to form interior and exterior space. Fischer von Erlach conceived of discrete spaces and masses that were added together to emphasize their individual nature. Hildebrandt's architecture, on the other hand, is more fluid and dynamic. He displayed an equal ability in handling mass composition and decorative detail. The exterior, regulated by architectural members, is a persuasive composition of convex and concave surfaces that is ultimately derived from ideas suggested by S. Agnese and S. Carlo in Rome. The centrally planned interior is composed of convex masses pushing in on the central space that escapes upward. A sense of dynamic space is heightened by the decorative scheme which restricts all fresco painting to the region above the entablature and all high intensity hues to the altars themselves.

Hildebrandt's masterfully composed Belvedere palace (1700–23) in Vienna was built for Prince Eugene of Savoy, the military hero of the sieges of Vienna and Turin. The palace façade (plates 86, 87) is composed of a large central block interrupted at the center by a triple arcade leading into the two-storied stair hall. The taller central block is flanked by wings ending in octagonal domed pavilions that punctuate and terminate the flat façade. Even here where Hildebrandt had a clear opportunity to break the composition into separate discrete units as Fischer was wont to do, the façade is a continuous flat plane converted by windows, frames, pediments, and pilasters into a richly patterned surface. The interiors are his most successful. The entrance to the palace is on the landing halfway between the lower garden floor and the main living floor. A pair of stairs leads up into the brightly lighted, but sparsely decorated, entrance to the main octagonal salon (plate 88). Hildebrandt was exceptional as a decorator and architect who could handle detail as well as the composition of large masses and spatial sequences. His ability to control both the decorative character and the architectural quality of his work made it extremely important for later architects.

In 1702 Jakob Prandtauer was called on to redesign the monastery at Melk on the Danube River. Melk was one of many

44

monasteries that, in a continuing medieval tradition, flourished during the late seventeenth and the eighteenth centuries in Austria. The monastic buildings dominate the river on top of a great pile of rock (plate 89). They were designed to be seen and appreciated from the river, and Prandtauer exploited the site to the fullest. The church itself thrusts upward through the monastic buildings, forming the culmination of the complex much as the medieval cathedral was the architectural climax of its town.

GERMANY

In Germany the High Baroque arrived later than in Austria but the two outstanding figures of the early eighteenth century, Matthaeus Daniel Pöppelman (1662–1736) and Johann Dientzenhofer (?–1726), were in some ways more advanced than their Austrian contemporaries.

Pöppelman was a favorite of Augustus the Strong, Elector of Saxony, one of the greatest baroque monarchs, and he was sent by him to study architecture in Paris, Prague, Vienna, Salzburg and Italy. In 1711 after his return to Dresden from Austria and Italy, Pöppelman built the Zwinger, a pleasure pavilion that is a noteworthy example in a long tradition of festival architecture and one of the high points of the German Baroque.

As first constructed (1709) the Zwinger was a wooden structure—a ceremonial amphitheater—and Pöppelman's task was to convert it to stone. The plan, much smaller than originally conceived, consists of a large, open square court about 350 feet on a side, with two wide and deep exedra, all enclosed by one-story wings. The wings are everywhere punctuated by taller pavilions, stairs, and balconies. Entrance pavilions (plate 90) at each of the cardinal points are fanciful combinations of Mannerist and Baroque elements. The extravagant two-storied open structure, crowned by a huge onion dome, concentrates all the masonry structure at the four corners in massive multiple piers that contrast strongly with the large, open, empty space at the upper level. The exuberant stair pavilion (plate 91) shows little or no concern for the structural nature of its forms—for example, the relation of arches to entablature or herms to pilasters—but there is a marvelous integration of decorative sculpture and architecture. Pöppelman conceived of his masses and spaces as separate entities and enlivened his forms with a kind of noisy vigor. But in these pavilions he also all but destroyed the wall—nothing is left but the piers themselves. In Germany it was in Pöppelman's work that the skeletalization of structure, one of the characteristics of the Rococo, began to be seen.

The longitudinal church attached to the Cluniac monastery at Banz in Northern Bavaria, attributed to Johann Dientzenhofer, is by far the most striking example of Franconian Baroque, and is noteworthy in the development of Rococo through the use of the transverse binding arch. Johann Dientzenhofer, who was probably trained by his father, an architect, is known to have traveled at least as far as Rome from whence he returned in 1699. He and the other members of his family worked in northern Bavaria and Bohemia, and it is still not clear which brother was responsible for certain buildings.

In spite of an unimaginative exterior, the Abbey Church at Banz (begun 1710) is, on the interior, a splendid adaptation of Guarini's Immaculate Conception in Turin. At Banz, Johann Dientzenhofer presaged the punctuated but synthesized space of the Rococo by stressing the longitudinal continuity of spaces. Transverse arches across the nave swing forward toward the altar or backward toward the entrance, touch at the crown, and subtly knit what are essentially separate, geometrically conceived spaces, into an interlaced whole of great vitality (plates 92, 93).

Swaying, binding arches similar to those at Banz were employed in the same year in a modified form at Breznov (near Prague) in St. Margaret's Church designed by Christoph Dientzenhofer, Johann's elder brother. The exploitation of this unusual feature culminated in the Rococo in the work of Balthasar Neumann (1687–1753). Curved binding arches became almost a distinguishing feature of his ecclesiastical work, and they are found in the Würzburg Hofkirche of 1733 (which he altered completely from Hildebrandt's original scheme), in the pilgrimage church of Vierzehnheiligen (1744), and in his last and perhaps best work, the Augustinian Abbey Church at Neresheim (1745).

Balthasar Neumann, the outstanding manipulator of space in eighteenth-century Germany, presented in his work a triumphant, ringing finale to a series of delightful variations on spaces first begun by Brunelleschi three hundred years earlier. In Würzburg the additions Neumann made to the *Residenz*, a suite of superb rooms, stairs, chapel, etc.—the urban palace of the building-mad Schoenborn family—are equally exciting (plate 94). The multiple spatial and light effects on the ground level are almost Piranesian fantasies made real (plate 95). Spaces seem to melt and merge into one another as light dissolves their substance, but, as one mounts the stairs, the multiplicity of view is replaced by a single, grand, immense space hovering above, into which the stair ascends.

The multiple spatial effects of Würzburg are even more thoroughly and more excitingly explored in Vierzehnheiligen and Neresheim. Vierzehnheiligen, the best-known of all German Rococo churches, has a checkered building history. In 1742 Neumann was called in to replace a local architect who had submitted designs for the church. The local architect was made supervisor of construction in Neumann's absence and, left with a free hand, altered the plans according to his own wishes. Neumann returned some time later (1744) and discovered the alterations made to his plans. The local architect was dismissed and Neumann supplied a supervisor from his own office. The work, however, was so far along that the plans had to be altered completely (plate 97). The church was finally completed after Neumann's death by his assistant.

The imposing but uninteresting twin-towered façade (plate 96) leads into a world of complex spatial delight. The exterior walls make up an almost boxlike rectangular shell enclosing a space that is cut and punctured, molded and warped, veiled and hidden by columns, piers, galleries, balconies, vaults, ribs, and arches that willfully join forces in a gigantic architectural game (plate 98). The only stable element remaining is the exterior wall and Neumann so pierces it with openings as virtually to destroy its planal continuity. The pilgrim leaves the normal "real" world when he enters Vierzehnheiligen. Walls no longer enclose—they are no longer massive and protective. Columns do not order stable, comprehensible spaces; the spaces themselves are both separated and interwoven. Lush architectural decoration, lavish altars and altarpieces, and densely ornamented, frescoed ceilings permeate the atmosphere (plate 99). It is no wonder the simple-minded German peasant has, for generations, felt this church to be the supreme expression of his religious belief. Neumann's fame rests upon the highly original character of his fluid interpenetrating spaces, his ability to destroy massiveness of structure even when working on a large scale, and his phenomenal ability to assimilate diverse architectural ideas from all over western and central Europe.

47

Johann Michael Fischer did not enjoy the same princely patronage as Neumann. He was primarily a church architect. His epitaph credits him with having built thirty-two churches and twenty-two monasteries. He was, apparently, an able administrator. The very best sculptors, painters, and decorators liked to work with him on his buildings where he encouraged them to produce their finest work. His interiors are, therefore, the most complete expression of the German Rococo. But the most successful Rococo exteriors in central Europe are also Fischer's, and the most exquisite example from them all is the majestic, austere façade of the parish church at Diessen (plate 100). Fischer, too, was concerned with the problem of mass, as was Neumann, but the bulkiness of mass was replaced by a sense of an easy, graceful flow of space that was controlled and ordered by slender columns, piers, and galleries. Fischer revealed the lightness of the skeletal structure by bathing it in light coming from hidden sources. Neumann also denied the mass of walls and even their structural necessity by skillfully arranging slender piers and columns in front of the direct glare of daylight entering through large openings. The strong light spills over the structural members and tends to subordinate them to space and light. Fischer and Neumann represent two outstanding but basically different solutions to the same problem—dematerialization of the fabric—in order to achieve diaphanous structure and spatial unity, the dream of all Rococo architects.

In the seventeenth and eighteenth centuries Western man felt he was part of a social structure to which he was subordinated. The Renaissance exaltation of the individual was replaced by the integration of the individual within society. In the arts the desire for an extensive synthesis was manifest in the subordination of individual parts of a composition to the whole as seen in the fusing of painting, sculpture, and architecture into a unit, and in the merging of individual buildings with the fabric of a city. But this was an integration of opposites. Perhaps the greatest discovery of the seventeenth and eighteenth centuries was the acceptance of a viable existence that included diverse opinions, intellectual contrasts, and even open strife. In our fragmented society there is renewed interest in the Baroque and Rococo age during which art, architecture, and the pageant of life were united in an appeal that reached and reflected all segments of society.

48

1. *S. Maria della Consolazione, Todi, begun 1508. Exterior.*

2. *Pietro da Cortona. SS. Martina e Luca, Rome, 1635–50. Exterior.*

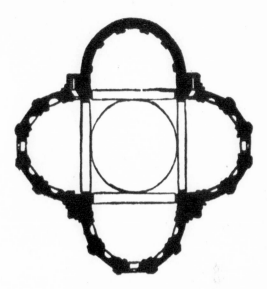

3. *S. Maria della Consolazione, Todi. Plan.*

4. *Pietro da Cortona. SS. Martina e Luca, Rome. Plan.*

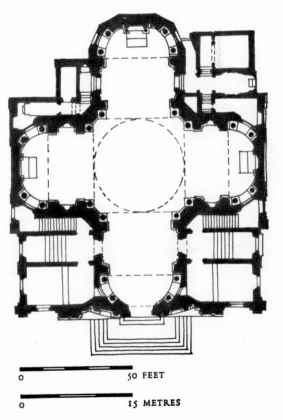

| | 50 FEET |
| | 15 METRES |

5. *S. Maria della Consolazione, Todi. Interior.*

6. *Pietro da Cortona. SS. Martine e Luca. Interior.*

7. *Bernardo Vittone. S. Chiara, Bra, begun 1742. Exterior.*

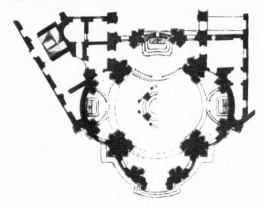

8. *Bernardo Vittone. S. Chiara, Bra. Plan.*

9. *Bernardo Vittone. S. Chiara, Bra. Interior.*

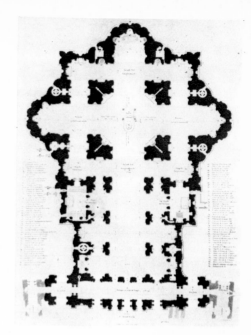

10. Carlo Maderno. *St. Peter's, Rome, 1606–12. Plan of nave and façade.*

11. Carlo Maderno. *St. Peter's, Rome. Nave.*

13. *Carlo Maderno. S. Susanna, Rome, 1597–1603. Façade.*

14. *Rome, St. Peter's Square c. 1638. Drawing by Israel Silvestre, detail.*

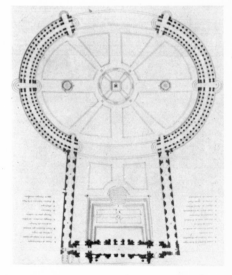

15. *Gian Lorenzo Bernini. St. Peter's Square, Rome, begun 1656. Plan.*

16. *Gian Lorenzo Bernini. St. Peter's Square, Rome. Colonnade.*

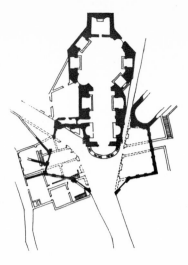

17. *Pietro da Cortona. S. Maria della Pace, Rome, 1656–57. Plan.*

18. *Pietro da Cortona. S. Maria della Pace, Rome. Façade.*

19. Gian Lorenzo Bernini. Palazzo Chigi-Odescalchi, Rome, begun 1664. Exterior.

20. Gian Lorenzo Bernini. S. Andrea al Quirinale, Rome, 1658–70. Façade.

21. Gian Lorenzo Bernini. S. Andrea al Quirinale, Rome. Interior.

23. Francesco Borromini. S. Carlo alle Quattro Fontane, Rome. Interior.

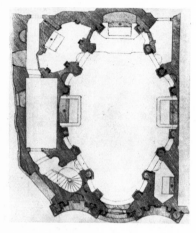

22. Francesco Borromini. S. Carlo alle Quattro Fontane, Rome, 1638–41. Plan.

25. Francesco Borromini. S. Ivo, Rome, 1642–50. View from courtyard.

26. Francesco Borromini. S. Ivo, Rome. Plan.

27.   *Francesco Borromini. S. Ivo, Rome. View up into dome.*

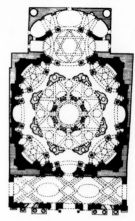

28.   Guarino Guarini. S. Lorenzo, Turin, 1666–79. Plan.

29.   Guarino Guarini. S. Lorenzo, Turin. Interior.

30. *Guarino Guarini. S. Lorenzo, Turin. View up into dome.*

31.   Guarino Guarini. Palazzo Carignano, **Turin**. 1679–92. Exterior.

32.   Guarino Guarini. Palazzo Carignano, **Turin**. Ground floor plan.

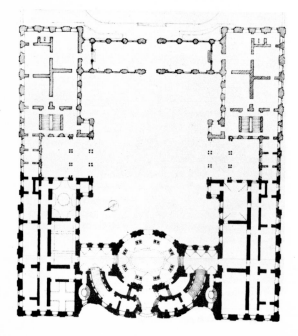

33.   Guarino Guarini. Palazzo Carignano, Turin. Main staircase.

34.   Guarino Guarini. Palazzo Carignano, Turin. Section through the main salon.

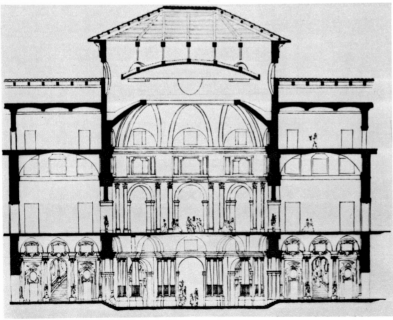

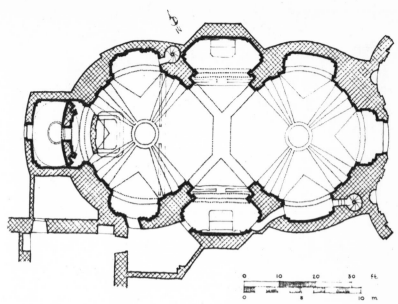

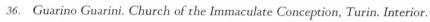

35. Guarino Guarini. Church of the Immaculate Conception, Turin. 1672–97. Plan.

36. Guarino Guarini. Church of the Immaculate Conception, Turin. Interior.

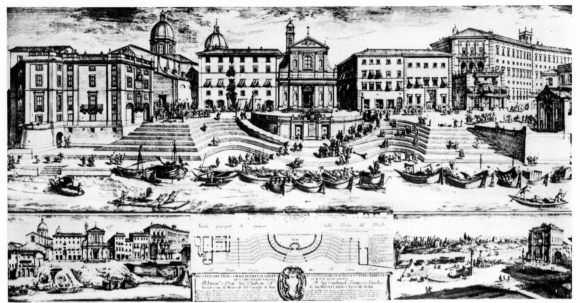

37.   *Alessandro Specchi. Porta di Ripetta, Rome, 1703 (now destroyed). From an engraving by A. Specchi.*

38.   *Alessandro Specchi and Francesco De Sanctis. Spanish Stairs, Rome, 1723–25.*

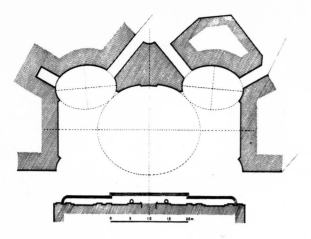

39.   *Filippo Raguzzini. Piazza S. Ignazio, Rome, 1727–28. Plan.*

41.   *Filippo Raguzzini. S. Maria della Quercia, Rome, begun 1727. Façade.*

40.   *Filippo Raguzzini. Piazza S. Ignazio, Rome.*

43. *Filippo Juvarra. Church of the Carmine, Turin, 1732–35. Interior.*

42. *Domenico Gregorini and Pietro Passalacqua. S. Croce in Gerusalemme, Rome, begun 1741. Façade.*

44.   *Filippo Juvarra. Stupinigi palace, 1729–33. Air view of complex of buildings.*

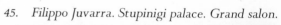

45.   *Filippo Juvarra. Stupinigi palace. Grand salon.*

46. Bernardo Vittone. S. Michele, Rivarolo Canavese. Exterior.

47.   Bernardo Vittone. S. Michele, Rivarolo Canavese. Interior.

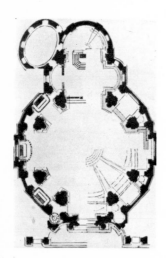

47a.   Bernardo Vittone. S. Michele, Rivarolo Canavese, begun 1759. Plan.

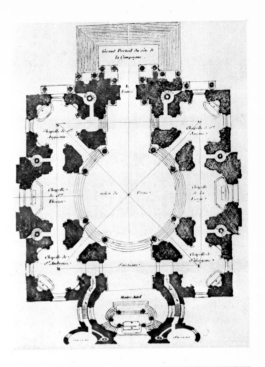

48. *Jules Hardouin Mansart. Church of Les Invalides,*
Paris, 1680–91. Exterior.

49. *Jules Hardouin Mansart. Church of Les Invalides, Paris. Plan and section.*

51. Jacques Lemercier. Church of the Sorbonne, Paris. Façade.

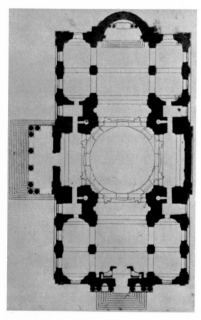

50. Jacques Lemercier. Church of
the Sorbonne, Paris, 1635. Plan.

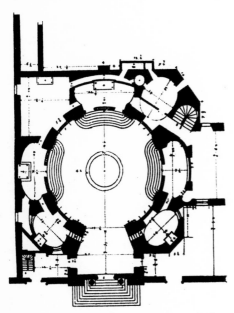

52. François Mansart. Ste. Marie de la
Visitation, Paris, 1632–34. Plan.

54.   François Mansart. *Château of Blois, Orléans Wing, 1635–38. Courtyard view.*

55.   *François Mansart. Château of Blois, Orléans Wing. View up main staircase.*

56.   François Mansart. Château of Maisons, 1642–46. Main entrance court.

57.   *Louis Levau. Collège des Quatre Nations, begun 1662. Engraving by Israel Silvestre.*

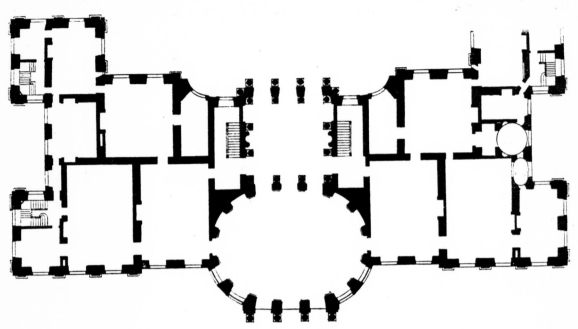

58. *Louis Levau. Château of Vaux-le-Vicomte, 1657–61. Plan of ground floor.*

59. *Louis Levau and André Le Nôtre. Château and gardens of Vaux-le-Vicomte.*

60. *André Le Nôtre. Tuileries gardens, Paris, 1664–72. Engraving of plan.*

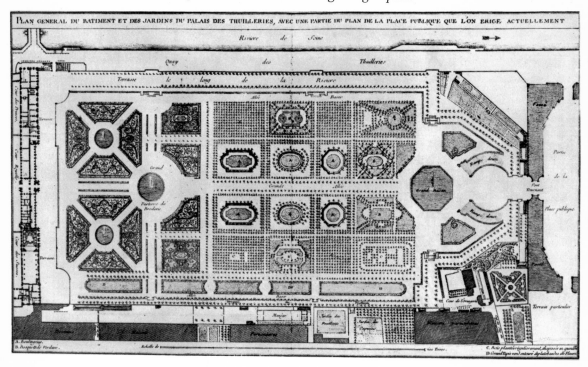

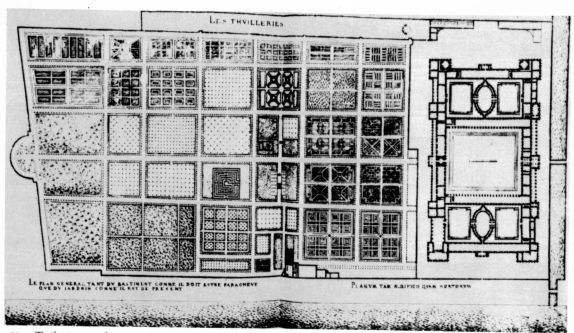

61. *Tuileries gardens in the late sixteenth century, Paris. Engraving of plan.*

62.   André Le Nôtre. Château of Versailles, begun 1667. Engraving of garden plan.

63.   André Le Nôtre. *Château of Versailles, begun 1667. View with gardens.*

64.   Louis Levau. *Château of Versailles, garden façade, begun 1669.* Engraving by Israel Silvestre.

65.   Louis Levau and Jules Hardouin Mansart. Château of Versailles, 1669–85. Garden-façade.

67. Gabriel-Germain Boffrand. Hôtel de Soubise, Paris, c. 1730. Salon Ovale.

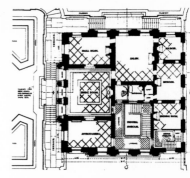

68. Jacques Ange Gabriel. Petit Trianon, Versailles, 1762–64. Plan of main floor.

69. Jacques Ange Gabriel. Petit Trianon, Versailles. Garden façade.

70. *Jacques Ange Gabriel. Place Louis XV, Paris, begun 1753. Engraving.*

71. *Emmanuel Héré de Corny. Place Louis XV, Nancy, 1751–59.* Air view.

72. *Emmanuel Héré de Corny. Place Louis XV, Nancy.* Plan.

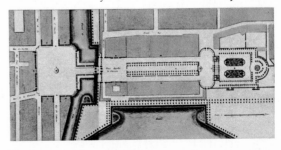

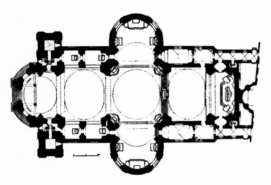

73. *Johann Michael Fischer. Benedictine Abbey, Ottobeuren, begun 1744. Plan.*

74. *Johann Michael Fischer. Benedictine Abbey, Ottobeuren. Exterior.*

75. *Johann Michael Fischer. Benedictine Abbey, Ottobeuren. Interior.*

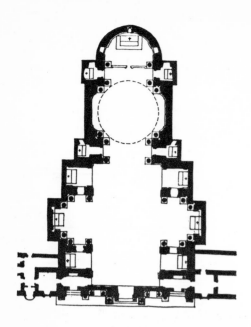

76. *Carlo Rainaldi. S. Maria in Campitelli, Rome, 1663–67. Plan.*

77. *Carlo Rainaldi. S. Maria in Campitelli, Rome. Interior.*

78. *Johann Michael Fischer. Benedictine Abbey, Ottobeuren. Interior.*

79.   *Bernardo Vittone. S. Maria di Piazza, Turin, 1751–68. Plan and section.*

80.   *Bernardo Vittone. S. Maria di Piazza, Turin. Dome over nave.*

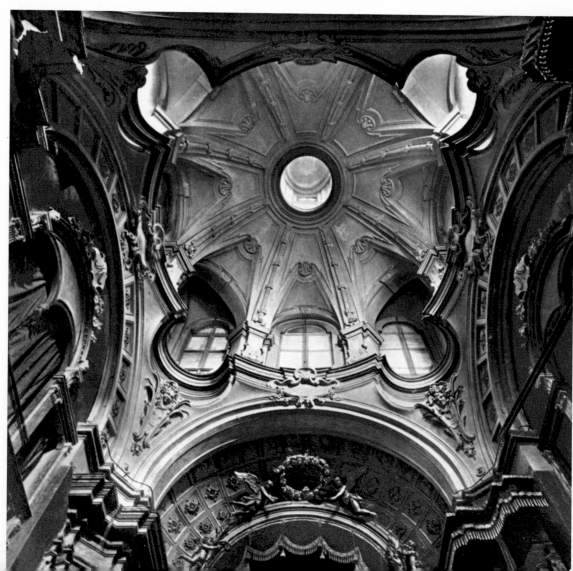

81. Bernardo Vittone. S. Maria di Piazza, Turin. Dome over choir.

82. *Johann Bernhard Fischer von Erlach. Karlskirche, Vienna, 1715–33. Exterior.*

83. *Johann Bernhard Fischer von Erlach. Karlskirche, Vienna. Plan.*

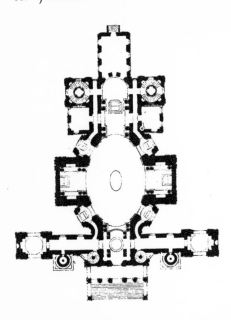

84. *Johann Lucas von Hildebrandt. Piaristen Church, Vienna, designed 1698, built 1715–21. Interior.*

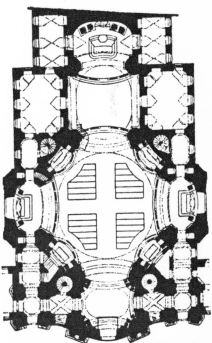

85. *Johann Lucas von Hildebrandt.
Piaristen Church, Vienna. Plan.*

86. Johann Lucas von Hildebrandt. Upper Belvedere, Vienna, 1700–23. Exterior detail.

87.   Johann Lucas von Hildebrandt. Upper Belvedere. Vienna, Exterior.

88.   Johann Lucas von Hildebrandt. Upper Belvedere, Vienna. Main stair hall.

89. *Jacob Prandtauer. Benedictine Abbey, Melk, begun 1702. View from the river.*

90.   Matthaeus Daniel Poppelman. Zwinger, Dresden, 1711–22. Entrance pavilion.

91.   Matthaeus Daniel Poppelman. Zwinger, Dresden. Stair pavilion.

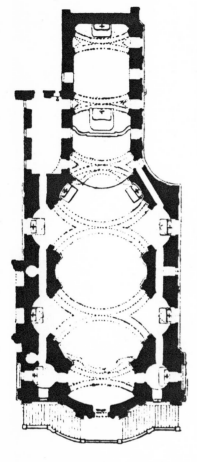

92. Johann Dientzenhofer.
Abbey Church, Banz,
begun 1710. Plan.

93. Johann Dientzenhofer. Abbey Church, Banz. Interior.

94. Balthasar Neumann. Residenz, Würzburg, 1719–44. Exterior.

95.   *Balthasar Neumann. Residenz, Würzburg. Main staircase.*

96.   *Balthasar Neumann. Pilgrimage Church, Vierzehnheiligen. Façade.*

SELECTED BIBLIOGRAPHY

SOURCES

Contemporary publications—A bibliography of seventeenth- and eighteenth-century books on architecture does not exist.

> *See however:*
> J. Schlosser-Magnino, *La Letteratura Artistica*, Florence, 1956 (VI, 3; VII; IX, 5).
> Leopold Cicognara, *Catalogo ragionato dei Libri d'arte e d'antichità posseduto dal Conte Cicognara*, Pisa, 1821.
> *Catalogue of Avery Memorial Library*, Columbia University, New York, 1958–59.

And for treatises that contain mathematical chapters on geometry and perspective:

> Pietro Riccardi, *Bibliografia Matematica Italiana*, Modena, 1870.

For Spanish books, in particular, see:

> F. J. Sanchez-Canton, *Fuentas literarias para la historia del arte español*, Madrid, 1923–41, Vols. II, III, IV, V.

Titles not in Schlosser include the following:

ITALY

G. A. Alberti, *Trattato della Misura delle Fabriche*, Venice, 1757.
—— *Istruzione pratiche per l'ingegnero civile*, Venice, 1799.
G. Amico, *L'architetto practico . . .*, Palermo, 1726.
F. Bibiena, *L'architettura civile*, Parma, 1711.
G. Fonda, *Elementi de Architettura Civile*, Rome, 1764.
G. Guarini, *Trattato di Fortificazione*, Turin, 1676.
C. Rana, *L'Alfabeto in Prospettiva . . .*, Turin (1780?).
F. Sanvitali, *Elementi de architettura civile*, Brescia, 1765.
B. A. Vittone, *Istruzioni Elementari*, Lugano, 1760.
—— *Istruzioni diverse*, Lugano, 1766.

FRANCE

P. Bullet, *L'Architecture Practique*, Paris, 1774.
S. Le Clerc, *Traité d'architecture*, Paris, 1714.
P. Le Muet, *Manière de bien Bastir . . .*, Paris, 1681.
J. Mauclerc, *Le Premier Livre d'Architecture*, Rochelle, 1600.
P. Nativelle, *Nouveau traité d'Architecture*, Paris, 1729.
R. Ouvrard, *Architecture Harmonique*, Paris, 1679.

ENGLAND

C. Campbell, *Vitruvius Britannicus*, London, 1715–25.
G. Gerbier, *Counsel and Advice to All Builders*, London, 1663.
J. Gibbs, *A Book of Architecture*, London, 1728.
W. Halfpenny, *Practical Architecture*, London (before 1724).

B. Langley, *The Builder's Jewel*, London, 1787.
I. Ware, *A Complete Body of Architecture*, London, 1756.

GERMANY

G. Boekler, *Architectura curiosa nova*, Nuremberg, 1664.
J. Penther, *Anleitung zur buergerlichen Baukunst*, Augsburg, 1746–64.

SOURCES

Publication of Documents

ITALY

C. Baroni, *Documenti per la storia dell'architettura a Milano nel rinascimento a nel barocco*. I: Edifico sacri, Florence, 1940.
V. Golzio, *Documenti artistici sul Seicento nell'archivio Chigi*, Rome, 1939.
J. A. F. Orbaan, *Documenti sul barocco in Roma*, Rome, 1920.
O. Pollak, *Die Kunsttätigkeit unter Urban VIII*, Vienna, 1927, 1931.
A. Baudi de Vesme, "L'arte negli stati sabaudi ai tempi di Carlo Emanuele I, di Vittorio Amedeo I, e della Reggenza di Christina di Francia," *Atti della società Piemontese di Archeologia e Belle Arti*, XIV (1923).

FRANCE

J. Guiffrey, *Les Comptes des Bâtiments du Roi sous le règne de Louis XIV, 1664–1715*, Paris, 1881–1901.
H. Lemonnier, *Procès Verbaux de l'académie d'architecture, 1671–93*, Paris, 1911–26.

GENERAL

HISTORICAL BACKGROUND

F. Braudel, *La Méditerranée et le monde méditerranéen à l'époque de Phillipe II*, Paris, 1949.
W. L. Dorn, *The Competition for Empire, 1740–63*, New York, 1940.
C. J. Friedrich, *The Age of the Baroque*, New York, 1952.
H. Nicolson, *The Agè of Reason*, New York, 1961.
F. L. Nussbaum, *The Triumph of Science and Reason, 1660–85*, New York, 1953.
D. Ogg, *Europe in the 17th Century*, 8th edition, London, 1960.
P. Roberts, *The Quest for Security 1715–40*, New York, 1947.
B. Willey, *The Eighteenth Century Background*, Boston, 1961.
—— *The Seventeenth Century Background*, London, 1942.
J. B. Wolf, *The Emergence of the Great Powers 1685–1715*, New York, 1951.

DEFINITIONS AND INTERPRETATIONS

E. Battisti, *Rinascimento e Barocco*, Turin, 1960.
G. Briganti, "Barocco, strana parola," *Paragone*, I (1950) 1.
—— "Barock in Uniform," *Paragone*, I (1950) 3.
—— "Milleseicentotrenta, ossia il barocco," *Paragone*, II (1951) 13.
E. Castelli, *Retorica e Barocco* (Atti del III Congresso Internazionale di Studi Umanistici), Rome, 1955.
L. Grassi, *Barocco o no*, Milan, 1953.

W. Hausenstein, *Vom Genie des Barock*, Munich, 1956.

B. C. Heyl, "Meanings of Baroque," *Journal of Aesthetics and Art Criticism*, XIX (1961).

Journal of Aesthetics and Art Criticism, V (1946); XII (1954); XIV (1955). Entirely devoted to Baroque problems with articles by various authors.

A. Riegl, *Die Entstehung der Barockkunst in Rom.*, Vienna, 1908.

R. Stamm (ed.), *Die Kunstformen des Barockzeitalters*, Munich, 1956.

V. Tapie, *The Age of Grandeur*, New York, 1960.

G. Weise, "L'Italia e il problema delle origini del 'Rococo,'" *Paragone*, V (1954), 49.

H. Wölfflin, *Renaissance und Barock*, Munich, 1888.

GENERAL HISTORIES

M. S. Briggs, *Baroque Architecture*, London, 1913.

A. E. Brinckmann, *Die Baukunst des 17. and 18. Jahrhunderts in den romanischen Ländern*, Berlin, 1915.

V. Golzio, *Il Seicento e il Settecento*, Turin, 1950.

C. Gurlitt, *Geschichte des barockstiles, des rococo und des klassicismus in Belgien, Holland, Frankreich, England*, Stuttgart, 1888.

F. Kimball, *The Creation of the Rococo*, Philadelphia, 1943.

M. Osborn, *Die Kunst des Rokoko*, Berlin, 1929.

H. Rose, *Spätbarock*, Munich, 1922.

A. Schmarsow, *Barock und Rokoko*, Leipzig, 1897.

A. Schönberger and H. Soehner, *The Rococo Age*, New York-Toronto-London, 1960.

O. Siren, *China and Gardens of Europe in the 18th Century*, Stockholm, 1950.

S. Sitwell, *Southern Baroque Art*, London, 1924.

W. Weisbach, *Die Kunst des Barock*, Berlin, 1924.

ITALY

See primarily:

R. Wittkower, *Art and Architecture in Italy, 1600–1750*, London, 1958 (Bibliography pp. 389-407).

See also:

G. Argan, *L'architettura barocca in Italia*, Milan, 1957.

G. Chierici, *Il palazzo italiano dal secolo XVII al XIX*, Milan, 1957.

G. Delogu, *L'architettura italiana del Seicento e del Settecento*, Florence, 1935.

D. Frey, *Architettura Barocca*, Rome-Milan, 1926.

C. Gurlitt, *Geschichte des Barockstiles in Italien*, Stuttgart, 1887.

J. Lees-Milne, *The Baroque in Italy*, London, 1959.

E. Mâle, *L'art religieux de la fin du XVIe siècle, du XVIIe siècle et du XVIIIe siècle*, Paris, 1951.

F. Milizia, *Memorie degli architetti antichi e moderni*, 4th edition, Bassano, 1785.

L. von Pastor, *History of the Popes*, Vols. XX-XL, St. Louis, 1950–53.

C. Ricci, *Architettura barocca in Italia*, Bergamo, 1912.

ROME

L. Callari, *I Palazzi di Roma*, 3rd edition, Rome, 1944.

A. Colasanti, *Case e Palazzi barocchi di Roma*, Milan, 1913.

A. De Rinaldis, *L'arte in Roma dal Seicento al Novecento*, Bologna, 1948.

K. Escher, *Barock und Klassizismus. Studien zur Geschichte der Architektur Roms*, Leipzig, 1910.

V. Fasolo, "Classicismo romano nel Settecento," *Quaderni* (1953), No. 3.

T. H. Fokker, *Roman Baroque Art*, Oxford, 1938.

C. d'Onofrio, *Le fontane di Roma*, Rome, 1957.

J. De Rossi, *Insignium Roma Templorum*, Rome, 1684.

G. K. Sutton, "Roman Façades in the 18th Century," *Connoisseur*, CLXI (1958).

J. Weingartner, *Römische Barockkirchen*, Munich, 1931.

PIEDMONT

A. E. Brinckmann, *Theatrum Novum Pedemontii*, Düsseldorf, 1931.

M. Passanti, *Architettura in Piemonte*, Turin, 1945.

A. Ressa, "L'architettura Religiosa in Piemonte nei secoli XVII e XVIII," *Torino*, July 1941.

INDIVIDUAL ARTISTS AND BUILDINGS

BERNINI:

P. Askew, "The Relation of Bernini's Architecture to the Architecture of the High Renaissance and of Michelangelo," *Marsyas*, V, 1950, pp. 39-61.

H. Brauer and R. Wittkower, *Die Zeichnungen des Gianlorenzo Bernini*, Berlin, 1931.

P. Fréart de Chantelou, *Journal du Voyage du Cavalier Bernin en France* (ed. by Louis Lalaune), Paris, 1885.

S. Fraschetti, *Il Bernini*, Milan, 1900.

R. Pane, *Bernini architetto*, Venice, 1953.

Piazza S. Pietro:

H. Brauer and R. Wittkower, *op. cit.*, pp. 64-102.

V. Mariani, *Significato del portico berniniano di S. Pietro*, Rome, 1935.

H. Millon, "An early 17th century drawing of the Piazza San Pietro," *Art Quarterly*, XXIV (1961).

R. Wittkower, "Il terzo Braccio del Bernini in Piazza S. Pietro," *Boll. d'Arte*, XXXIV (1949).

O. Zunica, *La piazza San Pietro e i Borghi*, Tivoli, 1937.

Palazzo Chigi-Odescalchi:

H. Brauer and R. Wittkower, *op. cit.*, p. 127.

A. Schiavo, *La Fontana di Trevi*, Rome, 1956.

T. Ashby, "The Palazzo Odescalchi in Rome," *Papers of the British School at Rome*, VIII (1916).

S. Andrea al Quirinale:

H. Brauer and R. Wittkower, *op. cit.*, pp. 110 ff.

BORROMINI:

G. C. Argan, *Borromini*, Verona, 1952.

E. Hempel, *Francesco Borromini*, Vienna, 1924.

P. Portoghesi, *Quaderni* (1953, 1954, 1955), Nos. 4, 6, 11.

—— *Palladio*, IV (1954).

—— "Borromini decoratore," *Boll. d'Arte*, XL (1955).

—— "Saggi sul Borromini," *Quaderni* (1958), Nos. 25-29.

H. Sedlmayr, *Die Architektur Borrominis*, 2nd edition, Munich, 1940.

H. Thelen, *70 Disegni di Francesco Borromini*, Rome, 1958 (Catalogue of exhibition at Gabinetto Nazionale delle Stampe).

S. Carlo alle quattro fontane:

P. Portoghesi, *Quaderni* (1954), No. 6.

H. Thelen, *op. cit.*, p. 11, *et passim.*

S. Ivo:

L. Benevolo, "Il temo geometrico di S. Ivo della Sapienza," *Quaderni* (1953)ᵗ No. 3.

S. Giannini, *Opera del Caval. Borromino cavata dai suoi originali, cioè la Chiesa e Fabrica della Sapienza . . .*, Rome, 1720.

A. Muñoz, "Il Palazzo e la chiesa della Sapienza," *L'Urbe*, II, fasc. 10, 1937.

P. Tomei, "Gli architetti del Palazzo della Sapienza," *Palladio V*, 1941, pp. 270-282.

PIETRO DA CORTONA:

N. Fabbrini, *Vita del Cav. Pietro da Cortona*, Cortona, 1896.

V. Moschini, "Le architetture di Pietro da Cortona," *L'Arte*, XXIV (1921).

A. Muñoz, *P. da Cortona*, Rome, 1921.

SS. Martina e Luca:

G. Giovannoni, "La Chiesa di S. Luca e il suo restauro," *La Reale Insigne Accademia di S. Luca* (Boll.). Rome, 1934, pp. 19-25.

GUARINO GUARINI:

A. E. Brinckmann, *Von Guarini bis Balthasar Neumann*, Berlin, 1932.

D. Coffin, "Padre Guarino Guarini in Paris," *Journal of the Society of Architectural Historians*, XV (1956), pp. 3-11.

G. Guarini, *Architettura Civile*, Turin, 1737.

P. Portoghesi, *Guarino Guarini*, Milan, 1956.

T. Sandonini, "Il Padre Guarino Guarini modenese," *Atti e memorie della Reale Deputazione di Storia Patria delle Provincie Modenesi e Parmensi*, Ser. 3, V (1888).

S. Lorenzo:

L. Denina and A. Proto, "La Reale Chiesa di S. Lorenzo in Torino," *Architettura Italiana*, XV (1920).

S. Giedion, *Space, Time and Architecture*, Cambridge, Mass., 1954.

Palazzo Carignano:

G. Chevalley, "Il Palazzo Carignano a Torino," *Boll. della Società Piemontese di Archeologia e Belle Arti*, V (1921), pp. 4-14.

Church of the Immaculate Conception:

R. Rigotti, "La chiesa dell'Immacolata Concezione ora cappella Arcivescovile in Torino," *Boll. della Società Piemontese di Archeologia e Belle Arti*, XVI (1932).

JUVARRA:

C. Rovere, V. Viale, A. E. Brinckmann, *Filippo Juvara*, Turin, 1937.

A. Telluccini, *L'arte dell'architetto Filippo Juvara in Piemonte*, Turin, 1926.

Carmine:

V. Mesturino, "Restauro della Chiesa della Carmine in Torino," *Boll. d'Arte,* XXXIV (1949).

Stupinigi:

M. Passanti, "La Palazzina di Caccia a Stupinigi," *L'Architettura,* III (1957).
M. Bernardi, *La Palazzina di Caccia di Stupinigi,* Turin, 1958.

MADERNO:

N. Caflish, *Carlo Maderno,* Munich, 1934.
U. Donati, *Carlo Maderno,* Lugano, 1957.
H. Egger, *Carlo Maderno's Projekt für den Vorplatz von San Pietro in Vaticano,* Leipzig, 1928.

PASSALACQUA:

M. Accascina, "Pietro Passalacqua architetto messinese a Roma," *Archivio storico messinese,* L-LI (1949–50).

RAINALDI:

E. Hempel, *Carlo Rainaldi,* Munich, 1919.
R. Wittkower, "Carlo Rainaldi and the Roman Architecture of the Full Baroque," *Art Bulletin,* XIX (1937), pp. 242-313.

SPECCHI:

T. Ashby and S. Welsh, "Alessandro Specchi," *The Town Planning Review,* XII (1927).
C. Bandini, "La scalinata e Piazza di Spagna," *Capitolium,* VII (1931).
E. Hempel, "Die Spanische Treppe, ein Beitrag zur Geschichte der Römischen Stadtbaukunst," *Festschrift H. Woelfflin,* Munich, 1924.
P. Pecchiai, *La scalinata di piazza di Spagna,* Rome, 1941.

RAGUZZINI:

M. Loret, "L'architetto Raguzzini e il rococo in Roma," *Boll. d'Arte,* XXVII (1933–34).
A. Neppi, "Aspetti dell'architettura del Settecento a Roma," *Dedalo,* XIII (1933).
M. Rotili, *Filippo Raguzzini e il Rococo Romano,* Rome, c. 1951.

VITTONE:

C. Baracco, "Bernardo Vittone e l'architettura guariniana," *Torino,* 1938, pp. 22-27.
A. Cavallari-Murat, "L'architettura Sacra del Vittone," *Atti e Rassegna Technica della Società degli ingegneri e degli architetti in Torino,* N.S. X (1956).
H. Millon, "Bernardo Antonio Vittone," *Architectural Review,* CXXIX (1961).
E. Olivero, *Le opere di Bernardo Antonio Vittone,* Turin, 1920.
P. Portoghesi, *Bernardo Antonio Vittone,* Milan, 1961.

Bra, Santa Chiara:

A. E. Brinckmann, *Theatrum . . ., op. cit.,* pp. 21-22.
E. Olivero, *op. cit.,* pp. 81-82.
R. Wittkower, *Art and Architecture . . ., op. cit.,* p. 285.

Turin, S. M. di Piazza:

A. E. Brinckmann, *Theatrum . . ., op cit.* pp. 72-73.

P. Cottino, *Cenni Storici sulla parrocchia di S. Maria di Piazza*, Pianezza, 1920.
E. Olivero, *op. cit.*, pp. 86-87.
R. Wittkower, *Art and Architecture* . . . p. 285-86.

Rivarolo Canavese, S. Michele:

A. E. Brinckmann, *Theatrum* . . . *op. cit.*, pp. 49-50.
E. Olivero, *op. cit.* pp. 95-96.

FRANCE

See primarily:
Sir R. Blomfield, *A History of French Architecture, 1494–1661*, London, 1911.
—— *A History of French Architecture, 1661–1774*, London, 1921.
A. Blunt, *Art and Architecture in France, 1500–1700*, Harmondsworth, 1953 (Bibliography pp. 291-296).
L. Hautecoeur, *Histoire de l'Architecture Classique en France*, Paris, 1943–55 (Vols. I-2; II - 1 and 2; III; IV; and V).
P. Lavedan, *French Architecture*, Harmondsworth, 1956.
See also:
B. Champigneulle, *Le Règne de Louis XIV*, Paris, 1943.
P. Du Colombier, *Le Style Henry IV—Louis XIII*, Paris, 1941.
E. Dacier, *L'Art au XVIIIe Siècle en France* . . ., Paris, 1951.
P. Francastel, "Baroque et Classique: une civilisation," *Annales*, 1957.
Louis Hautecoeur, *De L'Architecture*, Paris, 1938.
S. F. Kimball, *The Creation of the Style Louis XV*, New York, 1941.
Pierre Patte, *Monuments érigés à la gloire de Louis XV*, Paris, 1765.
P. Verlet, *Le Style Louis XV*, Paris, 1946.
R. A. Weigert, *Le Style Louis XIV*, Paris, 1941.

PARIS

F. Contet, *Les Vieux Hôtels de Paris*, Paris, 1909–30.
G. Pillement, *Les Hôtels de Paris*, Paris, 1945.

INDIVIDUAL ARCHITECTS AND BUILDINGS

GABRIEL

E. Fels, Comte de, *Ange-Jacques Gabriel*, Paris, 1912.
G. Gromort, *Jacques-Ange Gabriel*, Paris, 1933.

Le Petit Trianon:

James Arnott and John Wilson, *Petit Trianon*, New York, 1913.
Bernard Champigneulle, *Les Trianons*, Paris, 1948.
G. Desjardins, *Le Petit Trianon*, Versailles, 1885.

HÉRÉ DE CORNY

M. P. Morey, *Notice sur la vie et les oeuvres d'Emmanuel Héré de Corny*, Paris, 1863.

Nancy

André Hallay, *Nancy*, 3rd edition, Paris, 1920.
Anon., *Compte Général de la dépense des Edifices et Bâtiments que le roy de Pologne, Duc de Lorraine et Bar a fait construire pour l'embellissement de la ville de Nancy depuis 1751 jusqu'en 1759*, Lunéville, 1761.

LE NÔTRE

J. Guiffrey, *André Le Nôtre* (Grandes Artistes), Paris, n.d. (c.1911).

Gardens

Lucien Corpechot, *Parcs et jardins de France*, Paris, 1937.
E. Ganay, "Fabriques aux jardins du XVIIe siècle," *Gazette des Beaux Arts*, 1955.
George Gromort, *L'Art des Jardins*, 2nd edition, Paris, 1953.
Alfred Marie, *Jardins français classiques des XVIIe et XVIIIe siècles*, Paris, 1949.

F. MANSART

Anthony Blunt, *François Mansart*, London, 1941.

Château de Maisons

Leon Deshairs, *Le Château de Maisons*, Paris, 1907.
J. Stern, *Le Château de Maisons*, Paris, 1934.

Château de Blois

J. La Saussaye, *Histoire du Château de Blois*, 2nd edition, Paris, 1875.
P. Lesueur, *Le Château de Blois*, Paris, 1921.

VERSAILLES

C. Mauricheau-Beaupré, *Le Château de Versailles et ses Jardins*, Paris, 1924.
—— *Versailles, l'Histoire et l'Art*, Paris, 1949.
Pierre de Nolhac, *La Création de Versailles*, 2nd edition, Paris, 1925.

AUSTRIA AND GERMANY

See primarily:
   J. Bourke, *Baroque Churches of Central Europe*, London, 1958.
   C. W. Hegemann, *Deutsches Rokoko*, Königstein im Taunus, 1956.
   W. Pinder, *Deutscher Barock*, Königstein im Taunus, 1953.
   N. Powell, *From Baroque to Rococo*, London, 1959.
   M. Wackernagel, *Die Baukunst des 17. und 18. Jahrhunderts in den germa-nischen Ländern*, Berlin, 1919.
See also:
   R. Benz, *Deutscher Barock*, Stuttgart, 1949.
   A. Brinckmann, *Von Guarini bis Balthasar Neumann*, Berlin, 1932.
   A. Chroust, H. Hantsch, A. Scherj, *Quellen zur Geschichte des Barocks in Franken unter dem Einfluss des Hauses Schönborn...*, Augsburg, 1931–1955.
   G. Dehio, *Geschichte der Deutschen Kunst*, Vol. 2, 4th edition, Berlin-Leipzig, 1933.
   S. Giedion, *Spätbarocker und Romantischer Klassizismus*, Munich, 1922.
   C. Gurlitt, *Geschichte des Barockstiles und des Rokoko in Deutschland*, Stuttgart, 1889.
   W. Hager, *Die Bauten des deutschen Barocks*, Jena, 1942.
   S. Sitwell, *German Baroque Art*, London, 1927.

AUSTRIA:
   B. Grimschitz, *Wiener Barock Paläste*, Vienna, 1947.
   G. Jellicoe, *Baroque Gardens of Austria*, London, 1932.
   H. Riehl, *Barocke Baukunst in Österreich*, Munich, 1930.
   H. Sedlmayr, *Österreichische Barockarchitektur, 1690–1740*, Vienna, 1930.

GERMANY:

W. Boll, *Baukunst des Barock und Rokoko in Deutschland*, Munich, 1931.

P. Du Colombier, *L'Architecture française en Allemagne au XVIIIe Siècle*, Paris, 1956.

A. Feulner, *Bayerisches Rokoko*, Munich, 1923.

H. Franz, *Die Deutsche Barockbaukunst Mährens*, Munich, 1943.

H. Granz, *Studien zur Barockarchitektur in Böhmen und Mähren*, Brünn-Munich-Vienna, 1943.

M. Hauttmann, *Geschichte der kirchlichen Baukunst in Bayern, Schwaben und Franken 1550–1780*, Munich, 1921.

W. Hege & G. Barthel, *Barockkirchen in Altbayern and Schwaben*, Munich and Berlin, 1938.

H. W. Hegemann, *Die Deutsche Barockbaukunst Böhmens*, Munich, 1943.

N. Lieb, *Barockkirchen zwischen Donau und Alpen*, Munich, 1953.

H. Popp, *Die Architektur der Barock- und Rokokozeit in Deutschland und der Schweiz*, Stuttgart, 1913.

E. Redslob, *Barock und Rokoko in den Schlössern von Berlin und Potsdam*, Berlin, 1954.

INDIVIDUAL ARCHITECTS AND BUILDINGS

DIENTZENHOFER:

H. G. Franz, *Die Kirchenbauten des Christian Dientzenhofer*, Brünn-Munich-Vienna, 1942.

H. Schmerber, *Beitrage zur Geschichte der Dientzenhofer*, Prague, 1900.

O. Weigmann, *Eine Bamberger Baumeisterfamilie . . .*, Strasbourg, 1901.

FISCHER VON ERLACH:

G. Kunoth, *Die Historische Architektur Fischers von Erlach*, Düsseldorf, 1956.

H. Sedlmayr, *Johann Bernhard Fischer von Erlach*, Vienna, 1956 (Bibliography pp. 299-316).

Vienna, Karlskirche:

Greger, *Karlskirche*, Vienna, 1934.

J. M. FISCHER:

F. Hagen-Dempf, *Der Zentralbaugedanke bei Johann Michael Fischer*, Munich, 1954 (Bibliography pp. 105-106).

P. Heilbronner, *Studien über Johann Michael Fischer*, Munich, 1934.

Ottobeuren:

J. Beer, *Ottobeuren*, Königstein im Taunus, n.d. (c. 1957).

HILDEBRANDT:

B. Grimschitz, *Johann Lucas von Hildebrandt*, Vienna, 1959.

NEUMANN:

M. H. von Freeden, *Balthasar Neumann; Leben und Werk, Gedächtnisschau 1953*, Residenz Würzburg-Mainfränkisches Museum, Würzburg.

F. Knapp, *Balthasar Neumann, der grosse Architekt seiner Zeit*, Bielefeld-Leipzig, 1937 (44 pp.).

C. von Lorck, *Balthasar Neumann*, Berlin-Königsberg-Leipzig, 1940.

H. Reuther, *Die Kirchenbauten Balthasar Neumanns*, Berlin, 1960.

T. A. Schmorl, *Balthasar Neumann, Räume und Symbole des Spätbarocks*, Hamburg, 1946.

R. Teufel, *Balthasar Neumann; Sein Werk in Oberfranken*, Lichtenfels, 1953.

Würzburg:

M. H. von Freeden, *Würzburgs Residenz und Fürstenhof zur Schönbornzeit* (Mainfränkische Hefte), Würzburg, 1948.

—— *Quellen zur Geschichte des Barocks in Franken unter dem Einfluss des Hauses Schönborn*, Vol. II, Würzburg, 1951.

R. Sedlmaier and R. Pfeister, *Die Fürstbischöfliche Residenz zu Würzburg*, Munich, 1923.

Neresheim:

G. Neumann, *Neresheim* (edited by H. Jantzen), Munich-Pasing, 1947.

Vierzehnheiligen:

R. Teufel, *Vierzehnheiligen*, Lichtenfels, 1957.

PÖPPELMAN:

H. Heckmann, *M. D. Pöppelmann als Zeichner*, Dresden, 1954 (Bibliography, pp. 119-120).

Zwinger:

H. Hettner, *Der Zwinger in Dresden*, Leipzig, 1874.

PRANDTAUER:

H. Hantsch, *Jakob Prandtauer, der Klosterarchitekt des Österreichischen Barock* (Bibliography pp. 111-125), Vienna, 1926.

Melk:

F. Klauner, *Die Kirche von Stift Melk*, Vienna, 1948.

URBAN DESIGN

R. Blomfield, *A History of French Architecture, 1494–1661*, London, 1911.

—— *A History of French Architecture, 1661–1774*, London, 1921.

A. E. Brinckmann, *Baukunst des 17. und 18. Jahrhunderts in den Romanischen Ländern*, Potsdam, 1919.

G. Giedion, *Space, Time, and Architecture*, 3rd edition, Cambridge, Mass., 1954.

P. Francastel, "Versailles et l'architecture urbaine au XVIIe siècle," *Annales*, X (1955).

F. Hiorns, *Town Building in History*, London, 1956.

P. Lavedan, *Histoire de l'urbanisme*, Vol. 2, Paris, 1952.

L. Mumford, *The Culture of Cities*, New York, 1938.

C. Tunnard, *The City of Man*, New York, 1953.

P. Zucker, "Space and Movement in High Baroque City Planning," *Journal of the Society of Architectural Historians*, XIV (1955).

—— *Town and Square from the Agora to the Village Green*, New York, 1959.

INDEX

Numbers in regular roman type refer to text pages; *italic* figures refer to the plates.

SOURCES OF ILLUSTRATIONS

Alinari, Rome: 1, 5, 11, 12, 18, 19, 23, 24, 40, 42, 45

Alinari-Anderson, Rome: 2, 13, 20, 25, 38

Wayne Andrews, New York: 56

Archives Photographiques, Paris: 50, 51, 53, 55, 63, 65, 67, 69, 71

James Arnott and John Wilson, *Petit Trianon* (New York, 1913): 68

T. Ashby and S. Welsh, "Alessandro Specchi," *Town Planning Review*, XII (1927): 37

J. F. Blondel, *Architecture Française* (Paris, 1752–56): 60, 62

A. Blunt, *Art and Architecture in France, 1500–1700* (Harmondsworth, 1953): 49, 52, 58

Lorenzo Bricarelli, Turin: 47

J. Burckhardt, Gesammelte Werke, II, *Die Baukunst der Renaissance in Italien* (Basel, 1955): 3

Deutsche Fotothek, Dresden: 90

J. A. Ducerceau, *Livre d'Architecture* (Paris, 1559): 61

Courtesy of the Fogg Art Museum, Harvard University, Cambridge, Mass. (Gift of Mr. and Mrs. Philip Hofer): 14

T. H. Fokker, *Roman Baroque Art* (Oxford, 1938): 22, 39

Compagnia fotocelere, Turin: 31

Gabinetto Fotografico Nazionale, Rome: 6, 41

Giajetto, Turin: 36

B. Grimschitz, *Wiener Barock Paläste* (Vienna, 1947): 85

Leo Gundermann, Würzburg: 94

Walter Hege, Munich: 100

Photo Henrot, Paris: 66

O. Hoever, *Vergleichende Architekturgeschichte* (Munich, 1923): 83, 92

A. F. Kersting, London: 16

P. Letarouilly, *Le Vatican et la Basilique de Saint-Pierre de Rome* (Paris, 1882): 10, 15

N. Lieb, *Barock Kirchen zwischen Donau und Alpen* (Munich, 1953): 73

Mainfränkisches Museum, Würzburg: 97

Foto Marburg, Marburg-Lahn: 21, 48, 77, 93

Metropolitan Museum of Art, New York: 57, 64, 70

Henry A. Millon, Cambridge, Mass.: 23, 34; redrawn from G. Rigotti, *Boll. della Società Piemontese di Archeologia e Belle Arti*, XVI (1932): 35

Moncalvo, Turin: 7, 9, 44

Erich Müller, Kassel: 95, 96

Österreichische Nationalbibliothek, Vienna: 88

P. Patte, *Monuments érigés à la gloire de Louis XV* (Paris, 1765): 72

Augusto Pedrini, Turin: 43

P. Portoghesi, *Quaderni* (1958): 26

A. Renger-Patzsch, Wamel-Dorf über Soest-Westfalen: 91

Helga Schmidt-Glassner, Stuttgart: 54, 74, 75, 78, 82, 86, 87, 89, 98, 99

Soprintendenza ai Monumenti, Turin: 29, 30, 33, 46, 80, 81

John B. Vincent, Berkeley, California: 27

Roger Viollet, Paris: 59

B. A. Vittone, *Istruzioni diverse* (Lugano, 1766): 8, 47a, 79

Dr. Otto Winkler, Vienna: 84

R. Wittkower, *Art and Architecture in Italy, 1600–1750* (London, 1958): 4, 17, 28, 76

127

Printed in photogravure and letterpress by Joh. Enschedé en Zonen, Haarlem, The Netherlands. Set in Romulus with Spectrum display, both faces designed by Jan van Krimpen. Format by William and Caroline Harris.